REMEMBERING THE FALLEN 1914-1918

The guns had fallen silent. The fighting had ended. But, though the war had been won there were many who struggled to feel the sense of relief and joy that swept through the Allied nations.

As well as the hundreds of thousands left physically or mentally scarred by the fighting, those who most felt the pain of the five years of conflict included the friends and families of the dead. Figures realised by the British Government in 1920 revealed that 956,703 men and women had been killed or died whilst serving in the army, with a further 39,527 from the Royal Navy and RAF. With these statistics, it is perhaps unsurprising that the war touched literally every community throughout the country.

The end of the Great War ushered in a period of community and national commemoration and remembrance never witnessed before in the United Kingdom. From factories, schools and the smallest village, to individual regiments or whole cities, the sacrifice was marked by new memorials – even the few communities who suffered no loss, the so-called 'Thankful Villages', marked their good fortune.

This was the period when the newly-formed Imperial War Graves Commission began its remarkable work, the Poppy was adopted as a symbol of remembrance, the Last Post became known to everyone, the Unknown Warrior was buried in Westminster Abbey, and the battlefield tour, a pilgrimage for many of the grieving, gained prominence – all of which is explored in this unique insight into how the dead of the First World War were, and still are, remembered.

John Grehan
Editor

Editor: John Grehan
Design: Dan Jarman
Editorial Consultant: Paul Kendall (www.paul-kendall.co.uk)
Image Consultant: Robert Mitchell

Group CEO & Publisher: Adrian Cox
Commercial Director: Ann Saundry
Production Manager: Janet Watkins
Marketing Manager: Martin Steele

Contacts
Key Publishing Ltd
PO Box 100, Stamford, Lincolnshire, PE9 1XQ
E-mail: enquiries@keypublishing.com
www.keypublishing.com

Distribution: Seymour Distribution Ltd. Tel: 020 7429400
Printed by Warners (Midlands) Plc, Bourne, Lincolnshire.

The entire contents of this special edition is copyright © 2018. No part of it may be reproduced in any form or stored in any form of retrieval system without the prior permission of the publisher.

Published by Key Publishing Ltd.
www.britainatwar.com

○ A battlefield burial service underway on the Western Front.
(National Library of New Zealand)

REMEMBERING THE FALLEN 1914-1918 CONTENTS

◐ The ceremony for the unveiling of the Royal Artillery Memorial, by the Duke of Connaught, on 18 October 1925. The memorial, located at Hyde Park Corner, commemorates the 49,076 members of the Royal Regiment of Artillery who lost their lives in the First World War. (Historic Military Press)

CONTENTS

6 WE WILL REMEMBER THEM
Though the war had been won, there were many who struggled to feel the sense of relief and joy that swept through the Allied nations.

14 THE BOND OF SACRIFICE
One of the first of the national projects to commemorate the fallen was the Bond of Sacrifice.

18 BURYING THE DEAD
For those killed in action, whether or not they were afforded a fitting burial was often decided by circumstances.

24 STREET SHRINES
It was in the summer of 1916, during the Battle of the Somme, that the first Street Shrines made their appearance.

28 THE IMPERIAL WAR GRAVES COMMISSION
Thanks to the persistence of one man, an enormous scheme was devised to ensure that those who lost their lives in conflict would never be forgotten.

34 FINISHING THE TASK
With the land for cemeteries and memorials guaranteed, it was after the Armistice that the enormous task of recording the details of the dead began in earnest.

40 THE CENOTAPH
In 1920 the Cenotaph was designated as the United Kingdom's official national war memorial.

44 WAR MEMORIALS
How organisations and communities throughout the nation remembered the fallen.

◐ A Royal Marine and Royal Navy seaman provide a guard of honour as members of the public pay their respects at the Portsmouth War Memorial, which was unveiled on 15 October 1924. (Historic Military Press)

50 KNOWN UNTO GOD
On 11 November 1920, the body of an unidentified British soldier was buried, in the presence of the King, in Westminster Abbey.

56 A SYMBOL OF REMEMBRANCE
The poem *In Flanders Fields* helped ensure that the poppy was adopted as an international symbol of Remembrance.

63 THE KING'S PILGRIMAGE
In May 1922, King George V paid a personal tribute to the sacrifices of those who had given their lives in his name.

69 THE MENIN GATE
During the bitter fighting in the Ypres Salient the Menin Gate was one of the main routes used by Allied troops to reach the front.

76 THE BATTLEFIELD TOURISTS
In years after the First World War battlefield tourism began to flourish on an unprecedented scale.

4 REMEMBERING THE FALLEN

...NG THE FALLEN 1914-1918

A temporary wooden marker is prepared by a group of soldiers in preparation for being placed on the grave of a fallen comrade.

Three memorials on the top of the Butte de Warlencourt on the Somme. They commemorate the fallen of three battalions of the Durham Light Infantry – the 9th (on the left), 8th (centre), and, right rear, the 6th. The same three battalions of the Durham Light Infantry were later commemorated on the single wooden memorial seen here on the right - and which is today on display in Durham Cathedral. In the Autumn of 1926, at the request of the three battalions, it was brought to England and placed in the Memorial Chapel. *(Courtesy of Sara Mitchell)*

84 THE GREAT PILGRIMAGE
When the British Legion conceived of a mass pilgrimage of veterans to the Western Front it was on a vast scale.

88 THE FIELD OF REMEMBRANCE
Every year since 1928 a Field of Remembrance is opened in the grounds of Westminster Abbey.

90 A GREAT WAR 'BAYEUX TAPESTRY'
Among the more unusual forms of commemoration is the North Staffordshire Territorial Force's panoramic memorial canvas.

95 FROM PROPELLERS TO GLOBES
The commemoration of aircrew who died during the First World resulted in a number of unusual memorials.

103 THE THIEPVAL MEMORIAL
Towering over the landscape of the Somme battlefield, the Thiepval Memorial bears the names of more than 72,000 men who have no known grave.

108 A SECOND WORLD WAR
A selection of images that reveal how twenty years after the end of the Great War many memorials in Europe found themselves on the front line once again.

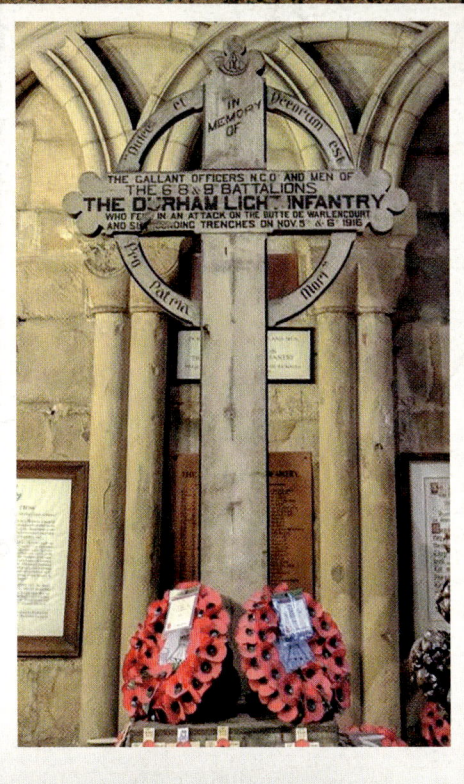

113 KEEPING THE NAMES ALIVE
Despite the passage of time, individuals and organisations continue to ensure that not a single sacrifice will be allowed to fade from memory.

REMEMBERING THE FALLEN 5

REMEMBERING THE FALLEN 1914-1918 WE WILL REMEMBER THEM

WE WILL REMEMBER THEM

The Armistice brought about an end to the fighting. However, though the war had been won, there were many who struggled to feel the sense of relief and joy that swept through the Allied nations.

The crowd held its collective breath as the minutes ticked by towards the deadline. Finally, the announcement was made that Great Britain was at war with Germany – and the crowds went wild. Shortly after 23.00 hours the King and Queen stepped out onto the balcony of Buckingham Palace. 'An enormous crowd collected outside the Palace ...' King George wrote in his diary of 4 August 1914. 'When they heard that war had been declared, the excitement increased and May and I with David [the Prince of Wales], went on to the balcony; the cheering was terrific.'

Similar scenes had been witnessed across Germany two days earlier at the news of the declaration of war against Russia. Likewise, in the Place de la Concorde, the Gare de l'Est and Gare du Nord in Paris as thousands of French Army reservists boarded trains taking them towards the border.

Across the United Kingdom, the recruiting stations were soon bursting with volunteers as young men flocked to fight for King and country – to fight and die. Few, if any, could possibly have imagined just how many men would die in the struggle that was to come, and the impact the war would have on the entire nation. While the Great War was the catalyst for much social change in both Britain and abroad, what affected families the most across the combatant nations was

WE WILL REMEMBER THEM REMEMBERIN

Times
AUGUST 5, 1914 1D.

BRITAIN AT WAR

○ Crowds gather near the House of Commons on the eve of war. The original caption states: "August 3, Bank Holiday, was a day of extraordinary national excitement. On Sunday the 2nd, a momentous Cabinet Council had been held, and on the afternoon of Bank Holiday, Sir Edward Grey stated British policy in regard to the violation of Belgian neutrality and the German invasion of France. 'We cannot stand aside,' he declared. "We cannot run away from our obligations of honour and interest with regard to the Belgian Treaty.' The mobilization of the Army immediately began, and so acute was the crisis that the Bank Holiday was extended for three days." (Historic Military Press)

○ A newspaper billboard detailing the momentous headlines on Tuesday, 4 August 1914. By the end of the day, seven European nations were at war.

the loss of so many friends, brothers, sons and husbands. The number of casualties has been repeated many times in many publications, and the totals are staggering, amounting to more than 41 million, of whom between 14 and 16 million were killed. Possibly the most disturbing of those shocking statistics, is that no one knows for certain the exact number of those killed – so many had died.

In terms of Great Britain, almost three-quarters of a million men lost their lives, affecting approximately 3 million families. In some communities from where the famous 'Pals' battalions were raised, almost an entire generation of young men was killed. For those who had lost sons it could mean a lonely and neglected old age; for those who lost husbands and boyfriends the post-war future was empty and bleak; for those who had lost fathers it often meant a childhood of hardship and struggle.

The post-war years were ones of great and widespread difficulty on many levels. The people for whom existence after the war was the most challenging was those servicemen who had suffered life-changing injuries. Around 2 million men were mentally or physically disabled, with approximately 40,000 having lost legs or arms and almost ➔

○ British soldiers on exercise in the summer of 1914 during the last days of peace. These men of the Honourable Artillery Company are pictured at Fargo Camp on Salisbury Plain. (Library of Congress; LC-B2-3394-5)

REMEMBERING THE FALLEN 7

REMEMBERING THE FALLEN 1914-1918 WE WILL REMEMBER THEM

process for hundreds of thousands of men and women was protracted and, for many, never truly fulfilled. This was even more pronounced for families and friends of those who had been listed as 'missing'.

This, to a large degree changed the attitudes to death and bereavement in Britain. According to Patricia Jalland, 'there was a complex shift from a Victorian culture where death was often accepted and grief openly expressed to a culture of avoidance, minimal ritual and private sorrow ... interwar England was obsessed with the cult of the dead in the face of widespread and harrowing bereavement. Victorian mourning practices seemed inadequate and inappropriate, particularly in the absence of most of the bodies of the fallen which had been buried on the battlefields.'[2]

◎ German troops on the move in Belgium whilst en route to the front in August 1914. (Library of Congress)

2,000 having been blinded.

The terrible conditions the men had to endure and consequence of the daily, even hourly, threat of death or disfigurement, had a profound effect upon the men who served on the front line. What was termed 'shell shock', and which today is recognised as post-traumatic stress disorder, manifested itself in a wide variety of symptoms, ranging from deafness, violent shaking and paralyses to anxiety, depression, hallucinations, delusions, flashbacks and nightmares. All too often it led to violence against wives and children, alcoholism or a failure to hold down a job.

In many respects these people also lost their lives, at least the lives they had before the war, and remembering their suffering is as much a part of the remembrance of all those for whom the war ended every dream. 'The interwar generation,' wrote Patricia Jalland, 'grew up in a bleak atmosphere of mass mourning'.[1]

That, though, was in the years ahead, and the immediate difficulty to be overcome by those left behind was to mourn for the lost ones; a process often made all the more difficult as from early 1915 the military policy of non-repatriation of war dead was strictly enforced and those who died at the front were buried in the countries in which they fell. This meant that many of those in mourning knew little of the circumstances in which their loved ones had died, that there was no funeral to celebrate the life so sadly taken, and no grave that could be visited until after the war. (and only then if funds were available). The mourning

◎ The first of many. Elements of the British Expeditionary Force head across the Channel to France – the first of many millions who would make the same journey, sometimes never to return, over the next few years. (Historic Military Press)

◎ Another image of men from the Honourable Artillery Company at Fargo Camp on Salisbury Plain in the summer of 1914. Following the declaration of war, such units would form the backbone of the United Kingdom's military response. (Library of Congress; LC-B2-3394-9)

WE WILL REMEMBER THEM REMEMBERING THE FALLEN 1914-1918

The occasional death in a community was part of the circle of life and families would receive the support and sympathy of those around them. But who could a mother turn to when her son had been killed when neighbours and friends had also lost their loved ones; when whole streets had lost their sons? The magnitude of the losses in the First World War were so enormous that personal grief of so many would have been overwhelming, thus it was collectivised, with 'ritualised' mourning which took physical shape in the form of town and village war memorials. There the dead could be remembered in a quiet and dignified way standing shoulder to shoulder with friends and neighbours. Their support was known and understood without comment. What could any of them say,

◯ A recruitment parade for Kitchener's Army in Bournemouth, Dorset, on 14 April 1915. (Historic Military Press)

◯ A tram that was used during a recruiting campaign for the 'Leeds Pals'. It is stated that this tram came to Morley in Leeds in September 1914 and was parked on the loop line by Morley Town Hall signing on recruits for much of the Great War. Unfortunately, after nearly two years training together many of these recruits met their deaths on the Somme in 1916. (Historic Military Press)

for they had all lost so much themselves? From those days onwards, reflective silence became an integral part of every subsequent commemoration.

There was also another side to the collective commemorations. Grief on such a scale had never been experienced before, and, to a large degree, needed explaining, or justification, if that grief was not to be turned into national outrage, as it did to a considerable degree in Germany. Politicians, church and community leaders had to find mechanisms which turned mourning into commemoration, even celebration. This was achieved by formalising the commemorations and turning them not merely into reverential wakes, but into grand affairs with service veterans marching in company with those of their battalion or regiment, led by booming brass bands, past clapping crowds. The veterans who marched in almost every town in Great Britain each November, regardless of wind or weather, became themselves a symbol of remembrance, helping to channel the sadness or anger of the bereaved families. Their lost ones were not merely mourned by a few close relatives but by hundreds, even thousands. The simple farm hand or factory worker, whose passing in peace time would go unremarked outside his close community, was celebrated in pomp and glory by multitudes and in particular by their comrades who had survived.

These events publicly declared the national gratitude for the sacrifice of lives on behalf of the state and are reinforced each year by the reigning monarch and a host of the highest dignities of the land by the laying of wreaths at the Cenotaph in Whitehall. Such displays raised the value of a lost life from that of a personal nature to that of a national one; the lowest private is awarded the same respect as the finest general. All are commemorated together. Anguish, heartbreak, agony, are transformed into pride. Life may have been lost, but the public displays powerfully transmit the message that the sacrifices made were not in vain.

This is why, on Remembrance Sunday in particular, the British nation does not just mourn its losses from the First World War but celebrates the achievements of those brave young men who paid the ultimate price to ensure the liberty and traditions of the nation continue to this day. This, to some degree, helped parents who had encouraged their children to volunteer to fight. This, in turn, led to a form of collective memory in which individual decisions were relegated, or transposed, to being societal ones. Their sons went to fight along with their pals and workmates. They all did. A decision shared is a decision halved. However, a grief-stricken Rudyard Kipling, whose only son was killed at Loos in 1915, could not unburden his personal guilt, when he wrote from the perspective of a young soldier: 'If any question why we died, Tell them because our fathers lied.'[3]

Family members are, of course, the ones most immediately thought of when

◯ Scottish troops, possibly of the 2nd Battalion Argyll and Sutherland Highlanders, pictured soon after their arrival in Boulogne on 14 August 1914. In the background is the Grand Hotel du Louvre et Terminus. (ww1images)

REMEMBERING THE FALLEN 1914-1918 WE WILL REMEMBER THEM

Soldiers tending the graves of fallen colleagues. (National Library of Scotland)

arch are inscribed the names of 54,896 men who have no known grave. When it was unveiled in 1927, Lord Herbert Plumer, who commanded V Corps at the Second Battle of Ypres and later the British Second Army, spoke these words:

'One of the most tragic features of the Great War was the number of casualties reported as "missing, believed killed".

'To their relatives there must have been added to their grief a tinge of bitterness and a feeling that everything possible had not been done to recover their loved ones' bodies, and give them reverent burial ... when peace came, and the last ray of hope had been extinguished, the void seemed deeper and the outlook more forlorn for those who had no grave to visit, no place where they could lay tokens of loving remembrance ... and it was resolved that here at Ypres, where so many of the missing are known to have fallen, there should be erected a memorial worthy of them which should give expression to the nation's gratitude for their sacrifice and their sympathy with those who mourned them.

considering the effects of the death of one of their kin, but frequently it was their comrades in arms who were even more profoundly affected, as one historian has found: 'Every frontline soldier experiences loss, the loss of comrades who were often intensely bonded with those who survived. The combination of this loss, often horrific and witnessed at close range ... produced a complex experience of bereavement, possibly even more intense than the loss of a close relative.'[4]

While it was the soldiers, sailors and airmen who died, it was those left behind who bore the legacy and it was those who also bore the burden of remembrance. Britain had begun to remember its dead while the war was still being fought with 'street shrines', the first of which was established in an East London street where sixty-five men had enlisted from forty houses. At the same time, the Imperial War Museum was established in 1917 specifically to commemorate the war.

Eventually, also, after the war, thanks to the efforts of the Imperial (later Commonwealth) War Graves Commission, friends and relatives were able to visit the beautifully created and cared-for graves of their loved ones in some far, foreign, but not forgotten, field, and for 'the missing' magnificent edifices were raised. One of the most magnificent of these structures is the Menin Gate Memorial to the Missing in the Belgium town of Ypres. As is explored in the pages that follow, upon this beautiful

Caring for the wounded. Dated November 1917, this image depicts one of the '2,000 wounded soldiers [who] recently visited the Leicester Palace Theatre; they were conveyed by over 400 motor cars'. (Historic Military Press)

> "One of the most tragic features of the Great War was the number of casualties reported as "missing, believed killed"."
> *Lord Herbert Plumer*

10 REMEMBERING THE FALLEN

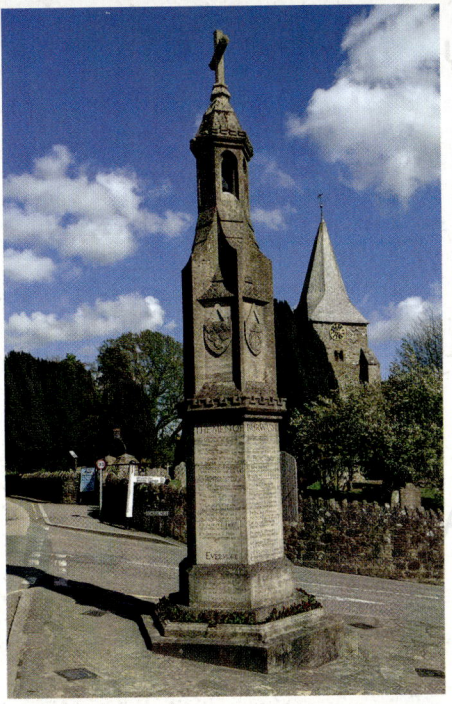

WE WILL REMEMBER THEM **REMEMBERING THE FALLEN 1914-1918**

Not all funeral services in the Great War were conducted on the same scale. This photograph depicts the state funeral of Field Marshal Frederick Sleigh Roberts, 1st Earl Roberts, VC, KG, KP, GCB, OM, GCSI, GCIE, KStJ, VD, PC. Roberts died of pneumonia at St Omer, France, on 14 November 1914, while visiting Indian troops fighting on the Western Front. After lying in state in Westminster Hall (one of two individuals who were not members of the royal family to do so during the 20th century, the other being Sir Winston Churchill), he was given a state funeral and was then buried in St. Paul's Cathedral. (Historic Military Press)

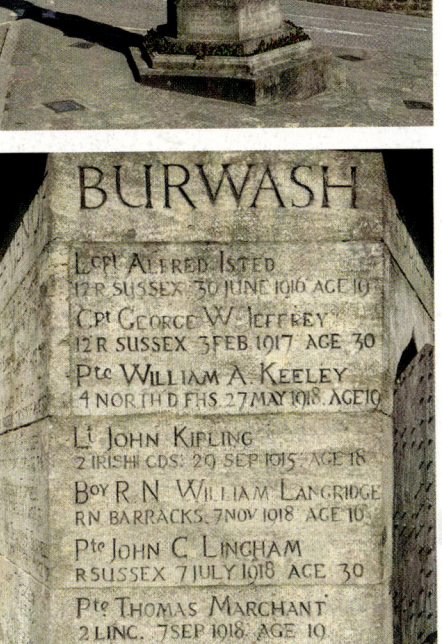

The war memorial in the East Sussex village of Burwash. Among the names carved on it is that of Lieutenant John Kipling, 2nd Battalion Irish Guards. John Kipling was the only son of the author Rudyard Kipling. He was killed on 29 September 1915, during the Battle of Loos, nearly six weeks after his eighteenth birthday. (Historic Military Press)

A memorial has been erected which, in its simple grandeur, fulfils this object, and now it can be said of each one in whose honour we are assembled here today … "He is not missing; he is here!'"

There were other buildings which, in their way, commemorated the men who had fought in the First World War. These were the network of special villages built for ex-servicemen and their families. These included Haig Homes in Welwyn Garden City, Westfield War Memorial Village in Lancaster and the Enham Village Settlement near Andover in Hampshire. These places were to help disabled servicemen, who because of their injuries were unable to return to their previous forms of employment, and their families.

These places still stand today, and in some cases, such as Lancaster's Westfield War Memorial Village, there is a waiting list of people that wish to move to the village, with priority still being given to families of war victims. There, each of the 113 properties in the village has a plaque outside the front door with information regarding a particular battle or an individual who fought in the First World War. In some instances, the plaques bear the names of those groups that helped to raise funds for the house to be built, as was the case with the first house built which bears the name of the man who donated the Westfield land to enable the concept to become reality, Herbert Lushington Storey.[5]

Troops of the 103rd (Tyneside Irish) Brigade, part of the 34th Division, pictured advancing from the Tara-Usna Line to attack the village of La Boisselle on the morning of 1 July 1916. This date, the start of the Battle of the Somme, has gone down in history as the single most destructive day ever experienced by the British Army. The 34th Division suffered heavier losses than any other British division that day. (Historic Military Press)

REMEMBERING THE FALLEN

REMEMBERING THE FALLEN 1914-1918 WE WILL REMEMBER THEM

As the 1914-18 conflict was so barbaric as well as being so deadly, it was generally believed that it would indeed be the war to end war and that those who had given their lives had also given the Western world peace. Their sacrifice had to be recognised. What they had done could not be forgotten or ignored. So, around the UK war memorials were erected in cities, towns and villages, with just a handful of 'Thankful' villages being spared the necessity of creating such monuments.

Those war memorials form a focal point for national commemorations each year and retain an importance and relevance even today. For they help the succeeding

⊕ An all-too-familiar sight by the end of the First World War – a battlefield burial marking the grave of another fallen soldier. This grave is of an unknown British soldier who was buried near Ginchy in September 1916. (NARA)

⊕ Members of the Women's Army Auxiliary Corps tending soldiers' graves at Abbeville, 15 September 1917. (NARA)

generation come to terms with the losses they have suffered in more recent conflicts, and they are commemorated collectively – a proud nation remembering the fallen of every era.

In recent years, grand artistic displays have added to the sense of gratitude expressed by the current generation, such as the *Poppies in the Tower* installation in London, which has become a travelling exhibition, and the remarkable interactive 'we're here because we're here' living memorial 'unveiled' to mark the centenary of the first day of the Battle of the Somme in July 2016; as well as the Step Short Memorial Arch in Folkestone created to mark the centenary of the end of the war. Alongside these, there have been a myriad of smaller but no less affecting community projects, which have seen schoolchildren born in the new century remember the dead in the company of senior citizens whose fathers fought in the war.

Nor is it just once a year, at the eleventh hour, on the eleventh day of the eleventh month, that the fallen are commemorated. For at the Menin Gate, at 20.00 hours, the Last Post is played every single day – and every single day crowds flock by the score to witness this moving tribute. Thanks to such events, we will, indeed, always remember them. ⊕

NOTES
1. Jalland, Patricia: Bereavement and Mourning (Great Britain), in: 1914-1918-online. *International Encyclopedia of the First World War*, ed. by Ute Daniel, Peter Gatrell, Oliver Janz, Heather Jones, Jennifer Keene, Alan Kramer, and Bill Nasson, issued by Freie Universität Berlin, Berlin 2014-10-08.
2. ibid.
3. From his poem, *Epitaphs of the War*.
4. Adrian Gregory, *The last Great War. British society and the First World War* (Cambridge University Press, Cambridge, 2008), p.19.
5. See: westfieldmemorialvillage.co.uk

⊕ The funeral of Lieutenant Colonel George Augustus King at Ypres on 17 October 1917. The Commanding Officer of the 1st Battalion, Canterbury Infantry Regiment, New Zealand Expeditionary Force (NZEF), King was killed when his headquarters was shelled five days earlier during the Battle of Passchendaele. He lies in the CWGC's Ypres Reservoir Cemetery. (Alexander Turnbull Library/National Library of New Zealand)

IMPORTANT NATIONAL ANNOUNCEMENT

Own the Official 2018 100 Poppies £5 Coin

SPECIAL OFFER £5 for £5 POSTFREE

Specifications: Country: Jersey, Year of issue: 2018, Metal: Cupro-nickel, Finish: Brilliant Uncirculated, Diameter: 38.61mm, Denomination: £5, Obverse: Ian Rank-Broadley, Reverse: Chris Lloyd

with a donation to The Royal British Legion

Act today- and you could own the new 2018 100 Poppies £5 coin for just £5 – POSTFREE. As a tribute to those who have made the ultimate sacrifice, a **brand new £5 Coin** has been issued for 2018 in support of The Royal British Legion.

Face Value Offer £5 for £5 POSTFREE

Yours for just £5, the focal point of this year's design is a stunning red poppy, which on closer inspection is made up of 99 individually engraved red ink poppies. This makes 100 poppies in total – a poignant number synonymous with the centenary year of the end of The First World War. **A donation from every coin sold will go directly to the Legion's work** and provide financial, social and life-long support to the Armed Forces community.

Supporting The Royal British Legion

Remember, you only pay £5, with a donation going directly towards the Legion's work. To order your coin today from The Westminster Collection, simply log on securely to **www.westminsterorders.com/WSR218P0**, call **0333 0032 777** or complete the Order Form below.

- **Yours for just £5 POSTFREE**
- **One year only 100 Poppies design**
- **A donation from each coin sold goes directly to The Royal British Legion**

Proud Supporters of The Royal British Legion

Official coins and medals have raised over £800,000 towards the work of The Royal British Legion

50p from the sale of this product will be paid to The Royal British Legion Trading Limited, which gives its taxable profits to The Royal British Legion (charity no. 219279) or Poppyscotland (Scottish charity SC014096). Your donation will be given to either charity depending on where the item was purchased.
For further information about The Royal British Legion please visit www.britishlegion.org.uk

Simply call **0333 0032 777** or log on to
www.westminsterorders.com/WSR218P0

Calls may be recorded. © 2018 The Westminster Collection - a trading division of 288 Group Limited :
Registered No. 2000413 : Russell House, Oxford Road, Bournemouth, BH8 8EX

FREEPOST ORDER FORM

Post to: The Westminster Collection : Freepost RSCR-JHCL-HBGT : PO Box 4848 : POOLE : BH12 9GB

✓ **YES** Please send me the 2018 100 Poppies £5 Coin(s) ordered below.

	2018 100 Poppies £5 Coin(s) for £5 each	
(max 3)	Postage and packing	FREE
	Total	

Order Ref: WSR/218P/0

☐ I enclose my cheque/P.O. payable to The Westminster Collection
☐ Please charge my Mastercard/Visa on despatch. My card no. is

EXPIRES M M Y Y

Your credit card will not be charged until your coin is despatched

Telephone No: (   )
(Please help us to keep you up-to-date with selected special offers)

Email address:
(Please help us to keep you up-to-date with selected special offers)

Signed:
(All orders must be signed and are subject to acceptance and status)

Mr/Mrs/Miss:

Address:

Postcode:

We think you'd be interested in some of the latest offers by post from our retail partners: companies operating in the clothing, collectables, food & wine, gardening, gadgets & entertainment, health & beauty, household goods and home interiors categories.
If you would prefer not to receive these, please tick this box [ ]
To learn more about our partners please see our privacy policy at www.westminstercollection.com/privacy

REMEMBERING THE FALLEN 1914-1918 THE BOND OF SACRIFICE

THE BOND OF SACRIFICE

Barely had the fighting begun when the thoughts of some turned to the question of commemorating the fallen. One of the first of the national projects to emerge was the Bond of Sacrifice.

Having disembarked at Boulogne on 14 August 1914, the men of the 4th Battalion, Middlesex Regiment soon found themselves moving east towards the front in Belgium. Seven days later, on the 21st, the battalion went into billets in the village of Bettignies south of Mons. Patrols were quickly sent out with instructions to try and locate the enemy. The men involved, which included Private L/14196 John Parr, who is described as a 'a reconnaissance cyclist', set off on bicycles that evening; they soon encountered German troops, reportedly in the area of Obourg.

Parr remained behind to monitor the enemy while a comrade pedalled back to battalion HQ to give a report. Nothing more was seen of Parr. The regimental history of the Middlesex Regiment states that although two platoons of 'D' Company were part of a brigade outpost line two miles north of Bettignies, the night of 21 August passed 'without incident'. The Commonwealth War Graves Commission records note that Parr 'was fatally wounded during an encounter with a German patrol two days before the battle [of Mons], thus becoming the first British soldier to be killed in action on the Western Front'.

It was not until the next day, however, that the first British Army officer would be killed in action fighting the Germans – but not on the Western Front. At the time of his death, 24-year-old Lieutenant George Masterman Thompson, 1st Battalion Royal Scots, was attached to the the Gold Coast Regiment, West African Frontier Force. The facts surrounding his death are detailed in his entry in Volume I of *The Bond of Sacrifice*:

'Having become Lieutenant in February, 1913, he went with his company to the coast, and after the declaration of war was for some days Military Commandant of the

○ Lieutenant Maurice James Dease VC, of the 4th Battalion, The Royal Fusiliers, was one of the first British officer battle casualties of the war and the first posthumous recipient of the Victoria Cross in that conflict. His VC actions were undertaken during the defence of the Nimy Bridge at Mons on 23 August 1914 – as depicted here. His biography appears on page 107 of Volume I of *The Bond of Sacrifice*. (Courtesy of David Rowlands; www.davidrowlands.co.uk)

14 REMEMBERING THE FALLEN

THE BOND OF SACRIFICE **REMEMBERING THE FALLEN 1914-1918**

○ This personal memorial to Lieutenant Maurice Dease VC (pictured on the right) was photographed on the railway bridge at Nimy. Dease's grave can be seen in St. Symphorien Military Cemetery. (Historic Military Press)

border town of Quittah ... On the 10th August he crossed over the border into the enemy territory of Togoland, and, leaving Lome on the 14th with the allied troops, marched, skirmishing in the rear, one hundred miles to Chra, where the Germans had concentrated their forces, and were strongly entrenched, with four Maxims and four hundred or five hundred rifles ...

'The following brief account was given by a correspondent of "the story of how at Chra, in German Togoland, an English Lieutenant and a little band of Senegalese died together":

'"Lieutenant Thompson, of the Gold Coast Regiment, with twenty-two British native troops, was placed on August 22nd at the disposition of Captain Castaing, of the Dahomey Brigade. To reinforce the little troop, of which the morale had been shaken by a preceding engagement, Captain Castaing added to it a Sergeant, two Corporals, and fourteen Tirailleurs.

'"At the very beginning of the fight the mixed section thus constituted found itself assailed by a sharp fusillade from strongly entrenched troops of the enemy, who had the further help of machine guns. It maintained an undaunted front, and four hours later, about half-past three in the afternoon, after the artillery had entered into action, Lieutenant Thompson, thinking the way sufficiently prepared, led his troop forward to push the attack to a finish. All the Castaing unit lent a vigorous support to him in this. But under the deadly hail of bullets the attack could not be carried beyond a point some fifty yards from the line of the enemy's trenches.

'"Lieutenant Thompson, mortally wounded, fell to the ground, and the British native troops wavered. But the Senegalese Tirailleurs, faithful to a long tradition of gallantry and faithfulness, refused to

○ Two French women tend the grave of Lieutenant Walter Evelyn Parke, 2nd Battalion Durham Light Infantry, who was killed in action on 13 October 1914. Parke, who was mentioned in French's despatch of 14 January 1915, appears on page 296 of Volume I of *The Bond of Sacrifice*. (Historic Military Press)

REMEMBERING THE FALLEN 15

REMEMBERING THE FALLEN 1914-1918 THE BOND OF SACRIFICE

abandon the body of the unknown leader their Captain had given them, and they succeeded in holding the ground they had won. When the enemy withdrew it was seen at what cost this ground had been kept. Side by side round the body of Lieutenant Thompson and an English native Sergeant lay the Sergeant, the two Corporals, and thirteen out of fourteen of the Tirailleurs … Lieutenant Thompson and his brave little band of Senegalese were buried together where they fell."'

In main, the work of three men, Colonel L.A. Clutterbuck, Colonel W.T. Dooner and Commander C.A. Denison, *The Bond of Sacrifice* is a biographical record of those British officers who fell in the First World War. As the editors themselves noted, 'The publication will be issued in volumes, each covering a period of, as nearly as possible, six months, and including the names of all Officers who lost their lives within that period from causes directly attributable to active service in the Great War. When doubt exists regarding the fate of an Officer, his name is not included until authentic confirmation of his death has been received. Special volumes are in course of preparation for the Royal Navy and for the Overseas Forces respectively, which it is intended to publish after the conclusion of the war.'

Volume I, in which Lieutenant Thompson appears, covers August to December 1914; Volume II January to June the following year. The first volume alone, the title of which was the suggestion of Rudyard Kipling, has biographies of some 1,400 men.

◯ Lieutenant Rowland Owen was serving in the 2nd Battalion, West Riding Regiment, when he was wounded and hospitalised at Boulogne in November 1914. Whilst recovering from his injuries, Owen wrote to the secretary of a football club he played for in Huddersfield: 'This year was going to be our great year. Well, so it is if we send as many men to the field of battle as we send to the field of play.' Published in the local press, Owen's letter inspired a drawing in a national weekly which became the basis of the recruiting poster 'Will They Never Come?'. Owen was killed in the fighting at Hill 60, and duly features on page 358 of Volume II of *The Bond of Sacrifice*.

Field Marshal the Viscount French of Ypres was asked to write the foreword to what he referred to as a 'deeply interesting volume': 'Its pages teem with deeds of gallantry and devoted self-sacrifice in the cause of King and Country. The brief and concise narrative which recalls the glorious ending of each separate life must appeal with simple and pathetic grandeur to every British heart.

'If we search for the many causes which have made for the British Army so magnificent a record, we will find amongst the most marked and prominent is the close and cordial relationship which has existed at all times between Officers and men.

'British soldiers have learnt from an experience which now covers centuries that in their Officers they possess leaders of indomitable courage, determination and self-reliance. A mutual confidence is established which has ensured many a glorious victory and often converted imminent defeat and disaster into a brilliant success. The Officers who have fallen in this great war have splendidly maintained these traditions. This is made abundantly evident to anyone who makes a study of the Rolls of Honour which have filled the columns of the daily paper.

'Enormous beyond all precedent as these death rolls have been it is a fact that the proportion of Officers to men is in excess of what it has been in any former war. Deep as must ever be the debt of gratitude which the Nation owes to its soldiers in the ranks, at least the same is owing to the devoted and intrepid leaders who have so freely sacrificed their lives on these blood-stained fields.'

As the war raged on, the scale of that sacrifice began to take its toll on *The Bond of Sacrifice*'s publishers and editors. As the casualty lists continually lengthened, it became clear that the project could not be sustained, with the result that there was never a third volume. ◯

◯ The Prince of Wales at the grave of Prince Maurice of Battenberg on 1 May 1923. Lieutenant Prince Maurice Victor Donald Battenberg, 1st King's Royal Rifle Corps, was killed in action on 27 October 1914, aged 23. The grandson of Queen Victoria, he was buried in Ypres Town Cemetery. His entry is on page 23 of Volume I. (Historic Military Press)

GUERNSEY STAMPS AND COLLECTABLES

GUERNSEY POST

New Issue: 8th November 2018

LIMITED EDITION OF 1918

Product range and pre-orders available for this issue from 22nd October

Stories from the Great War - Memorials

Limited Edition Great War Souvenir Folder

Comes with numbered summary card

As part of a five-year programme to commemorate the centenary of the First World War, we unearthed a wealth of information about the many men and women of the Bailiwick who stepped forward to serve for King and Country.

The last set in the series, to be issued on the 8th November this year, looks at the memorials created to honour the people of the Bailiwick who made the ultimate sacrifice. *It has been an honour to tell their stories.*

We have also produced a limited edition folder to house the complete set of stamps from our Great War series. A memorial in its own right, this souvenir folder lists the 1,500 brave individuals who fell during the conflict and also contains a miniature replica of the RGLI flag that hangs in the Town Church, St Peter Port, Guernsey.

Prestige Booklet available with 4 stamps per pane and detailed information about the collection

Order Guernsey & Alderney stamps online or by tel: +44 (0) 1481 716486;
email philatelic@guernseypost.com

Guernsey Stamps
@guernseystamps

www.guernseystamps.com

ARMISTICE
A Century Of Commemoration

156-page photographic tribute

JUST £7.99

THE DAY OF VICTORY
One hundred years since the guns fell silent, we look back at how a nation has commemorated the Great War

Featuring rare images from the Daily Mirror archives

ORDER: www.keypublishing.com/shop/armistice
CALL: 01780 480404   Lines open: 9am-530pm GMT. FREE P&P on all UK and BFPO orders.

879/18

REMEMBERING THE FALLEN 1914-1918 BURYING THE DEAD

BURYING THE DEAD

For those killed in action, be it in the air, at sea, or on the battlefields around the world, whether they were afforded a fitting burial was often decided by circumstances. There was also the longer-term issue of the care of their graves.

At 02.15 hours on 21 July 1916, the men of the 1st/1st Bucks Battalion, Oxford and Bucks Light Infantry, climbed out of their trench, named as Sickle Trench, on the Somme and struck out towards the German line. The attack that followed was a costly affair for the Bucks Battalion as four officers and eight other ranks were killed. A further 100 had been wounded, with another forty-two men missing. One of those who did not return was 29-year-old Captain Lionel William Crouch.

Some information concerning Lionel's last moments were detailed in a letter written by one of his comrades: 'The attack in which dear old Lionel was killed ... [was] in open country and at night. I mayn't tell you more.

He was hit by a machine-gun bullet, but was not killed at once, as he fell down and said to Wheeler, "I'm hit, Wheeler". Wheeler started to try to get him to a shell-hole, but was then hit in the arm himself, so he had only one arm to drag Lionel with.

'Lionel was hit again almost at once, and that seemed to be fatal, as he said "good-bye" to Wheeler several times, and then spoke no more, and Wheeler said he evidently died almost immediately after the second bullet. He doesn't think Lionel suffered very much, thank God. Wheeler then went back and reported that Lionel had been killed.'

Further details were provided by Private C.J. Wheeler, who was Lionel's batman. In a letter to Lionel's parents, Wheeler wrote:

'I can assure you he died bravely. He was leading and cheering his men on when he was hit with a bullet. I was dragging him back to a shell-hole when I was hit in the muscle of the right arm. I still tried to get him back, but could not do much with one arm, when he was shot again, this time through the stomach, and he died in about ten minutes. I laid with him until his death, and then took his maps and personal property he had on him.'

It would seem that Lionel's body lay unburied for six weeks before others could risk going into No Man's Land, as the regimental Chaplain, Kenneth Jackson, informed his mother in a letter dated 30 August 1916: 'Yesterday I was up in that

○ **Part of the Somme battlefield photographed in 1917, after the offensive of the previous year had ended. More than 95,000 men lost their lives during the four months of the Battle of the Somme, one of whom was Captain Lionel William Crouch. He was buried in a battlefield grave similar to those seen here.** (Courtesy of the Australian War Memorial; P03631.216)

BURYING THE DEAD REMEMB

The view looking out from the rear wall of the Commonwealth War Grave Commission's Pozieres British Cemetery near Ovillers-la-Boisselle into the general area of what would have been No Man's Land on the night of 20/21 July 1916. The attack by Lionel Crouch's men would have been made roughly from the left-hand side of the dark green field in the centre foreground. The German front line was to the right-hand side of this view. It is assumed that Lionel was killed in the area of this dark green field. (Historic Military Press)

Captain Lionel Crouch (front left) and his company officers pictured in May 1916. (Courtesy of Jon Cooksey)

part of the line where your son lost his life. There we found his body. We buried him where he lay, and we had a short service. A small cross now marks the spot.'

Lionel's brother, Guy, was subsequently able to find out a little more information concerning the burial service, as he described to his mother on 3 September: 'I have to-day been able to see the officer who was in charge of the burial party who found dear old Lionel and buried him. He says he knew who he was by his medal-ribbon, etc., and buried him near where he lay, and the padre who was with them read a short service over him. They put up a stick with his name, regiment, rank, and the date (July 21) on it (they had no crosses left), and also left a card in a shell case with the same particulars on it, in case the stick got displaced or obliterated. The whole thing was necessarily rather hurried, as the party was being shelled and one man was hit by shrapnel.'

Then, finally, on 14 November 1916, Guy was at last able to visit the resting place of his brother: 'I went up this morning and met a party of three men and a lance-corporal ... and we made up dear old Lionel's grave properly. The cross is of wood and has a Bucks Battalion cap badge let into the top, and the lettering is cut into the wood to make it permanent. The grave is in a hollow made by a shell, about 8 feet across and 1 foot deep. We made up the mound, and made an edging of cast-iron shell-cases, like this ... So the top of the mound is about level with the surrounding ground, and the 1-foot dip into the shell-hole makes a very good protection to the grave itself.'

Lionel Crouch had clearly meant a great deal to those who knew him and fought by his side, as the efforts taken to find his body and provide it with a suitable burial bear testimony. However, whilst he had been buried with as much reverence as was possible, the question still remained as to what would happen to his grave in the longer term.

FABIAN WARE

One of the first individuals to consider formalising the approach to the burial of the nations' battle casualties was Fabian Ware. Bristol-born Ware had trained as a school teacher, becoming an assistant headmaster at a number of secondary schools in the UK before taking up a position of Inspector of Schools for the Board of Education. He was appointed to the role of Assistant Director of Education in the Transvaal, later becoming Acting Director of Education for the Transvaal and the Orange River Colony and then Director of Education on the Transvaal Legislative Council. Ware had returned to England from Africa in 1905 and became editor of the *Morning Post*. Then, in another career change, Fabian Ware became a director of Rio Tinto Mining Company.

The men of the 1st/1st Bucks Battalion march through Chelmsford en route to their port of embarkation, bound for the Western Front, on 30 March 1915. (Courtesy of Jon Cooksey)

REMEMBERING THE FALLEN 19

REMEMBERING THE FALLEN 1914-1918 BURYING THE DEAD

◉ The site of Pozieres British Cemetery stands roughly on the spot where the line of Sickle Trench meets the main D929 from Albert to Pozières. From the spot where the photographer is standing, the trench from which Crouch and his comrades set off on their attack would have run north along the cemetery wall on the right. The British attackers formed up roughly along the left-hand edge of the dark green field in the foreground. The German front line, their target, was approximately 300 yards to the right.
(Historic Military Press)

◉ The wooden marker that was used on Lionel Crouch's original battlefield grave. The fact that his name has been engraved on it suggests that this was the marker put in place by his brother on 14 November 1916. Along with Lionel's medals, this wooden cross is on display today in the TA Centre in Oxford Road, Aylesbury.
(Courtesy of the Bucks Military Museum Trust)

At the outbreak of war, Ware had tried to join the British Army, but at the age of forty-five was rejected as being too old to fight. Nevertheless, he was determined to contribute in some way to the war effort and managed to join the British Red Cross in France. He used his influence to obtain a letter from the French Embassy in London authorizing him to take command of the Red Cross Mission in the Lille and Amiens district, a position he took up on 19 September 1914.

Establishing himself in the Hôtel d'Europe in Lille, Ware took over the Red Cross' Mobile Unit, or 'flying unit' as it was often called. This was a band of volunteer civilians, driving civilian vehicles. Officially, the Mobile Unit was under the control of the Joint War Committee of the British Red Cross Society and the Order of St John of Jerusalem. It was Lord Kitchener who had suggested that a mobile unit should be established to search for missing soldiers along the line of retreat between the rivers Aisne and Ourcq. Attached at first to the French I Cavalry Corps during the First Battle of Ypres, and later the French X Corps, the unit picked up numbers of wounded soldiers and transported them to hospitals.

Whilst he was in this role Ware became acutely aware of the lack of any official mechanism by which the graves of the fallen were recorded. As there was no official system in the British Army for recording graves at this stage of the war, as part of their service tending the wounded Red Cross members always tried to take note of where the dead had been buried in the hope that they would be able to inform relatives. Ware told his men to take very careful notes on the precise location of every grave and every cemetery and to even maintain the graves themselves so that they would not disappear in the hectic heat of battle.

There had never been a war in which there had been such an enormous number of casualties, and it was evident to Ware that unless some proper record was made across the battlefronts, the dead and the missing would be very quickly lost forever. Each day on the Western Front alone there were hundreds of casualties and during the big battles many thousands were killed or were missing. Ware saw that if action to preserve the graves was not taken quickly, his small unit would be overwhelmed and be unable to record every grave.

GRAVES REGISTRATION COMMISSION

The situation in the autumn of 1914 was summed up by Ware in the Introduction to his book *The Immortal Heritage*: 'In the clash and bewilderment of actual fighting, in the rapid ruin and chaos and oblivion of the front line with its enormous process of annihilation, perhaps not many soldiers retained the confidence that the dead – themselves, it might be tomorrow, or the next instant – would at length obtain some lasting and distinct memorial.

'Of course, the fighting man, from the earliest stages of the War, was familiar with attempts to give proper burial to those who were killed in action. There were well-known arrangements and orders concerned with this sad necessity; and a great deal was done by commanding officers and padres and the men under them in the forward areas. "Some frail memorial" was erected duly over

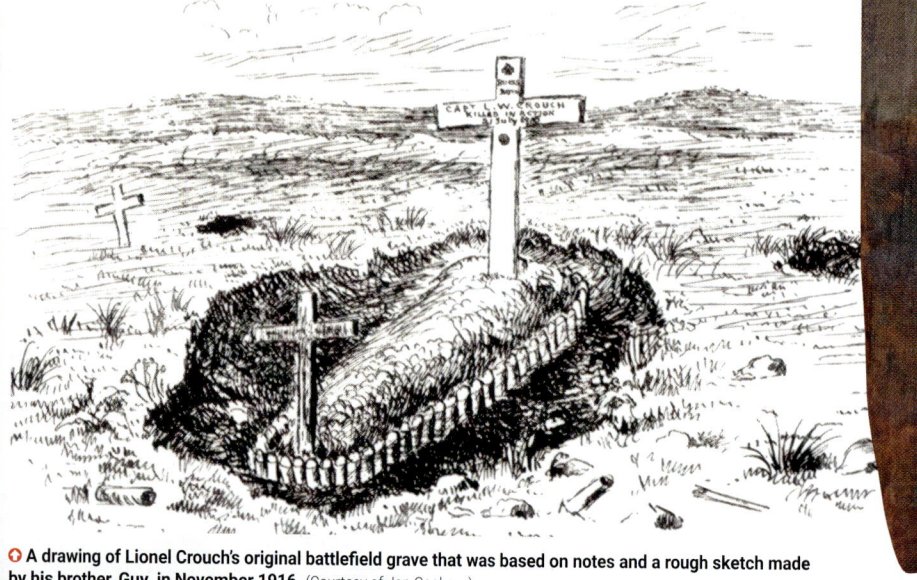

◉ A drawing of Lionel Crouch's original battlefield grave that was based on notes and a rough sketch made by his brother, Guy, in November 1916. (Courtesy of Jon Cooksey)

20 REMEMBERING THE FALLEN

BURYING THE DEAD REMEMBERING THE FALLEN 1914-1918

many and many a grave dug under fire. But the whole problem was vast and severe. Bombardment, which swelled month by month into a wider extent and a fiercer violence, appeared likely in the course of years to obliterate almost all separate burial. The assembly of wooden crosses in the wrecked villages near the line, with here and there an additional sign of remembrance suggested by the feeling and opportunity of surviving fellow soldiers, seemed to have poor chance of remaining recognizable or visible after one more outburst of attack or counter-burst, when high explosive and torrential steel would tear up the soil over deliberately chosen spaces of the land.'

In October 1914, the Red Cross' medical assessor, Lieutenant Colonel Edward Stewart, paid a visit to Ware's unit and

⊙ At some stage, Lionel's body was exhumed and concentrated in the nearby Pozieres British Cemetery, his grave marked today by a standard CWGC headstone. (Historic Military Press)

⊙ The man responsible for the formation of what is today the Commonwealth War Graves Commission, Major General Sir Fabian Arthur Goulstone Ware KCVO, KBE, CB, CMG. (Historic Military Press)

Ware took advantage of the opportunity not only to demonstrate his team's work with the wounded but also to show the graves of the fallen in a cemetery in Bethune. What Ware wanted to impress upon the lieutenant colonel was the temporary nature of the British graves, which were marked by a simple wooden cross, with the details of the dead serviceman marked on each one in pencil. It was evident that in time, such details would fade away and the remains of many men who had given their lives for their country would be forgotten.

Lieutenant Colonel Stewart was moved by Ware's work and he granted the Mobile Unit formal leave to properly register graves and to include details of those men listed as 'missing'. With this, each grave was given a permanent marker, was recorded in an official register and was placed on a maintenance schedule.

All of this struck a chord with the Adjutant-General of the BEF, Major General Sir Nevil Macready. The enormous, shocking loss of life during the early months of the war had led to growing public clamour for something to be done to preserve the lasting resting places of men lost in battle. Because of the scale of the losses, families were affected the length and breadth of the United Kingdom, indeed throughout the Dominions and Empire, and their voices could not be ignored. Macready, therefore, advised the Commander-in-Chief of the BEF to set up an organization within the British Army to mark and register every grave – and, of course, it was Ware's unit that was to run this operation. On 2 March 1915, this was officially sanctioned, with the establishment of the Graves Registration Commission.

To standardize the recording of the graves, Grave Registration Reports were produced, which detailed the particular burial site or ground, its name and map

"I can assure you he died bravely. He was leading and cheering his men on when he was hit with a bullet. I was dragging him back to a shell-hole when I was hit in the muscle of the right arm."

⊙ Canadian troops tending the battlefield graves of their comrades who fell in the fighting at Vimy, in June 1917. (Department of National Defence/Library and Archives Canada)

REMEMBERING THE FALLEN 21

REMEMBERING THE FALLEN

reference, and included basic information on the casualty, such as name, service number, rank, regiment, unit and date of death. In terms of cemeteries, where possible these records were listed in Plot, Row and Grave order.

These would be collated by an officer given responsibility for a certain battle sector. These Burial Returns would be sent off to headquarters where the information would be transposed onto two lists. The first list noted the graves by regiment and the second recorded the location. With Ware's team registering more than 31,000 graves between May and October of 1915 alone (this had reached the total of 50,000 by May 1916), the task of collecting and collating all the information was no easy task, as one of Ware's men, H. Broadley, explained: 'It frequently requires considerable patience and some skill as an amateur detective to find the grave of some poor fellow who has been shot in some out of the way turnip field and hurriedly buried, but I feel my modest efforts are amply rewarded when I return a day or two later with a wooden cross with a neat inscription and plant it at the head of his grave, for I have the proud satisfaction of knowing that I have done some slight honour to one brave man who has died for his country.'[1]

At this early stage, the Graves Registration Commission was still operating under the auspices of the Red Cross but attached to the British Army's Adjutant-General's office. That said, the efforts of the Commission were readily appreciated by the commander of the BEF's I Corps, General Douglas Haig, who wrote to the War Office shortly after the Commission had been established: 'It is fully recognized that the work of the organization is of purely sentimental value, and that it does not directly contribute to the successful termination of the war. It has, however, an extraordinary moral value to the troops as well as to the relatives and friends of the dead at home ... Further, on the termination of hostilities, the nation will demand an account from the government as to the steps which have been taken to mark and classify the burial places of the dead.'[2]

The idea that the government would be held accountable for the graves of its soldiers was a novel one, but Haig's observations indicate the direction in which the mood of the country was taking.

○ A British soldier tending a soldier's grave near Blangy, 3 May 1917, during the Battle of Arras. (Library of Congress)

○ The grave of a soldier from the Royal Sussex Regiment who was killed or died on the North West Frontier in India between March 1918 and November 1918. (Historic Military Press)

○ A farmer who has returned to his war-ravaged fields works around the remains of a British tank and, in the foreground, a battlefield grave, presumably a crewman from the tank. The latter, numbered *C-31*, awaits removal from the battlefield after the Armistice. The location is given at Frezenberg. (Historic Military Press)

NOTES
1. Quoted in Julia Summers, *Remembered, The History of the Commonwealth War Graves Commission* (Merrell, London, 2007), p.15.
2. Quoted in G. Kingsley Ward and Major Edwin Gibson, *Courage Remembered* (HMSO, London, 1995), p.45.

Watchmaker Col&MacArthur commemorates the Armistice of World War One and pays tribute to the fallen with a very special limited-edition watch

Col&MacArthur is built on a common passion for horology and founding values of pride, heritage and commemoration, something that's helped them become the official watch supplier for the British Army and the Royal Guards of Buckingham Palace.

The brand strongly believes that all of their watches must not only contain an elegant design and a robust technology but also tell a personal story for the person who wears and uses it.

The limited-edition *'Armistice 1918'* finds home in the **Legacy** collection. The watch was designed to commemorate the centenary of World War One and to honour the heroes who fought during the war.

The *'Armistice 1918'* watch is the ideal vehicle to acknowledge the passing of time and to assert the importance of remembrance. The watch also helps to set commemorative traditions. The motto of the Legacy collection, where the *'Armistice 1918'* watch will belong states 'Time flies, heritage remains.' Therefore, every detail of this watch is thoroughly thought out in order to commemorate the Armistice.

The design incorporates strong symbols of the end of the war including the poppy, the date 11·11·18 and the last soldier to be killed, Private George Edwin Ellison who was shot at 9:30am while scouting on the outskirts of Mons.

Also incorporated onto the front of the timepiece are the coordinates of the wagon, Compagnie Internationale des Wagons Lits, which had served as the mobile headquarters of the French Armed Forces, N°2419D, which is where the end of the war was formally agreed.

Col&MacArthur also offer engraving on the back of the watch; a permanent souvenir allowing the wearer to pay tribute to an ancestor or hero of their choice by honouring the fallen's sacrifice and memory, at any time. For those purchasing the watch as a gift for a loved one, a thoughtful personal message to the wearer can be engraved on the back. This final distinguishing feature completes the story told by the timepiece.

'Armistice 1918' is the first edition of the **Legacy** collection and we hope the first of a long series of successes" states Sébastien Colen, one of the founders of **Col&MacArthur.**

This unique limited-edition timepiece comes in a beautifully crafted wooden box and is available for £345 (with the option of engraving for £40) from www.colandmacarthur.com, in addition to a limited amount being on sale at the Mons City memorial museum, which stands in the location where Private George Edwin Ellison was killed.

The *'Armistice 1918'* watch is the perfect item for collectors with an interest in timepieces or those who wish to commemorate the war and soldiers who fought for our country or offering a nice watch as a Christmas present.

REMEMBERING THE FALLEN 1914-1918 STREET SHRINES

STREET SHRINES

With the majority of the fallen buried overseas, many of those at home looked for a way to commemorate the dead. It was in the summer of 1916, during the Battle of the Somme, that the first Street Shrines made their appearance.

It was in the summer of 1916, and in the East End of London, that a new form of commemoration and remembrance, the first Street Shrines, were erected to honour those men and women who had enlisted in the armed forces, and in particular those who had fallen in the service of their nation.

On 10 August 1916, these first Shrines were the subject of a royal visit. This was reported the following day in *The Times*: 'The Queen paid a visit yesterday afternoon to South Hackney and spent an hour or so inspecting a row of the street shrines … which South Hackney parish invented, and which other parishes, partly on the recommendation of the Bishop of London at the Diocesan Conference, are setting up. The Church's part is to hang somewhere in the street – usually on the wall of the house which has sent the most men to the Army and Navy – a framed and glazed roll of honour, bearing the names of all the men from that street who are

○ **A First World War Street Shrine that was placed on a wall in the St Paul's Mission District in the East End of London.** (Historic Military Press)

○ **The Street Shrine that was erected in Tatton Street, Salford, Lancashire.** (Historic Military Press)

24 REMEMBERING THE FALLEN

STREET SHRINES **REMEMBERING THE FALLEN 1914-1918**

serving with the forces, and round it some flower vases. The street does the rest.

'The street keeps the vases filled with flowers and adds more of its own. The street hangs up flags, the street puts among the flags and the flowers the photograph or bust of Lord Kitchener or some other great soldier, and photographs and other mementoes of the sons and husbands of whom it is justly proud. Photographs of these shrines are sent to men at the front, and the men at the front write back to express their pride at having their names thus honoured in their home parish and street.

'There are now nine such shrines in South Hackney, and others are being added. Practically every street which had houses flush with the pavement is to have one. Of these nine the Queen visited five; and those five marked the streets where the number of men who had voluntarily joined the forces exceeded the number of houses

⊙ The Queen inspects the Street Shrine in Balcorne Street on 10 August 1916. 'The streets of this teeming district have sent nearly 500 men to the Colours. To one mother, who has four sons at the Front, the Queen said: "Keep a brave heart!" and shook hands with her.' (Historic Military Press)

in the street. First came Palace-road – 70 houses, 111 men; then Havelock-road, then Frampton Park-road, then Eaton-place, and, finally, Balcorne-street.

'In Palace-road the Queen spoke with a mother who had four sons in the Army and has lost one; in Balcorne-street, too, she spoke with the mothers of four soldiers. At each shrine she left her carriage to stand on the pavement and look closely at the roll, the flowers, and the photographs.'

This was not the only visit undertaken by the Queen to Street Shrines in London. Her second tour was made on 2 October the same year: 'The Queen, in fulfilment of a promise made to the vicar of St. Peter's, Regent-square, spent some time in the parish yesterday viewing war shrines erected

⊙ The Queen pictured during her tour of Street Shrines in the East End on 10 August 1916. She is seen here 'in Palace Road, from which 111 men had voluntarily enlisted out of a total of 77 houses'. The original caption went on to add that 'this excellent system of recording local patriotism was instituted by the Rev. B.S. Batty, Rector of St John of Jerusalem, South Hackney'. (Historic Military Press)

by the residents. Driving slowly through the district, the Queen visited Compton-street, Wakefield-street, Harrison-street, Seaford-street, and Regent-square, and saw the various shrines erected there, mostly on the rails in front of the houses.

⊙ A surviving Street Shrine in Eton Street, Kingston upon Hull. Some of these stone or marble shrines are post-war replacements of original examples. (Courtesy of Bernard Sharp; www.geograph.org.uk)

'The houses had been hurriedly adorned with flags, and others were waved from the windows. On reaching Sidmouth-street, which possesses a shrine containing a roll of about a hundred names, the Queen was received by the vicar, the Rev. C.W. Stevens. She alighted and closely inspected the shrine, which was decorated with flags and flowers. The Queen placed on the shrine a bouquet of wall-flowers, forget-me-nots, and roses.'

Though the intention had originally been to erect such shrines on the walls of buildings in the poorer parts of London and at the entrances to places of worship, popular sentiment overwhelmingly approved of the idea, and people in towns and villages in all parts of the country soon sought their own examples. Driven by this increasing public demand, the *Evening News* arranged for an exhibition of the various designs available to be held at Selfridges on Oxford Street – as detailed, once again in *The Times*, on 31 October 1916:

REMEMBERING THE FALLEN **25**

REMEMBERING THE FALLEN 1914-1918 STREET SHRINES

The highly-decorated Street Shrine that was erected in Palace Road, Hackney. The original caption, dated 12 July 1916, states: 'Nowhere in London has the price of war been paid more freely than in the East. More than a hundred men, for instance, voluntarily enlisting from Palace Road, Hackney. Of these, many have already given their lives for King and Country. The names of men at the front are written in a framed Roll of Honour. To these little "shrines" women bring their offerings of flowers, and a brave note is struck by the flags with which the wall is decorated.' (Historic Military Press)

Below: Soldier's wives decorating the Roll of Honour at Hackney with fresh flowers—a daily ceremony in every street. Right centre: Collecting and carding hobnails to send out to the troops. This scene is in the Croydon clearing house. Right side below: Juvenile farm hands from Rickmansworth School planting potatoes.

A news cutting depicting what is believed to be the Street Shrine that was placed in Palace Road, South Hackney. The original caption states: 'Soldiers' wives decorating the Roll of Honour at Hackney with fresh flowers – a daily ceremony in every street.' (Historic Military Press)

Located on the wall of the Fox Inn in the village of Denchworth, near Wantage in Oxfordshire, this surviving Street Shrine lists thirty-one men from the village who served in the First World War, two of whom lost their lives. (Historic Military Press)

'The shrines are for the most part simple in design; there are panels for the framed Roll of Honour, a projecting canopy, and brackets for holding flowers on walls ... Artists have offered designs. Messrs. Bodley and Hare have executed for the *Evening News* a shrine in triptych form, with doors for the protection of panels from weather, at a cost of £14 10s., and this seemed to be the highest in the collection. Other designs ranged from 30s. upwards. A simple Gothic panel, shown by Mr. C. Geddings, of Hoddesdon, is adapted for production in plaster for 30s. in Portland cement it costs £3; in stone £5 10s., and in oak £6. The organizers of the exhibition will give a large number of the shrines to the poorer parishes.'

As the weeks passed, Street Shrines appeared in more and more locations. On 5 January 1917, for example, it was noted that 'the parish of St. Silas, Kentish-town (population 11,500), has 11 street War Shrines, inscribed with more than 1,200 names. A War Shrine bearing the names of 56 men who have fallen in the war has been placed at the roadside at Hale, near Farnham, Surrey.'

London, however, continued to be at the heart of the Street Shrine movement. On 26 February 1917, it was announced that further examples had been unveiled across the capital: 'General Sir Horace Smith-Dorrien unveiled at Christ Church, Westminster Bridge-road, on Saturday, tablets set in the outer wall recording the names of 730 men and boys from the district who have taken part, or are still taking part, in the campaign. Lady Jellicoe unveiled three war shrines at Battersea on Saturday, the first being at the old Parish Church.

Listing thirty-two names, of whom five were killed or died, this Shrine was originally erected in Chichester Road, Leytonstone. Having survived in situ for many decades, by 1993 it was in poor repair, the weather having exacted a heavy toll. The decision was therefore taken by the local community to move it inside, and it now hangs in St Margaret's Church in Woodhouse Road, Leytonstone, today. (Historic Military Press)

26 REMEMBERING THE FALLEN

STREET SHRINES REMEMBERING THE FALLEN 1914-1918

◦ A contemporary postcard showing the Street Shrine that was located on the wall of a building in Crabb Street, Rushden, Northamptonshire. (Historic Military Press)

◦ Protected from the elements, this Great War Street Shrine is located on a wall in Sharp Street in Kingston upon Hull. (Courtesy of Bernard Sharp; www.geograph.org.uk)

'During the ceremony Sergeant J.H. Taylor, of the Battersea Battalion, Royal West Surrey Regiment, was presented by the Mayor with the DCM, which was afterwards pinned on by Lady Jellicoe. A procession was then formed to St. Mary-le-Park Church, and afterwards to the corner of Orbet-street, and Octavin-street, where the two other shrines were unveiled. Lady Beatty yesterday unveiled outside St. Thomas's Church, West Ham, a war shrine, containing the name of its vicar's son and 39 other men of the parish killed in action.'

On 14 July 1917, the papers reported that, 'A war shrine made of oak, with a large cross of beaten copperwork in the centre, provided by the contribution of residents at Hampton Court, has been placed on the outer wall of the Palace entrance near the Trophy Gates. It bears the names of 64 men who have fallen in the war. Lady White, widow of Field-Marshal Sir George White, unveiled the shrine yesterday.'

In August 1918, while the Hundred Days Offensive was raging, a large Shrine was erected in Hyde Park. In the first week alone, some 100,000 people visited it, with 200,000 flowers left there in just ten days.

Street Shrines even appeared as far away as the Channel Islands when the Guernsey parish of St Peter Port erected its own example in January 1917. Consisting of a walnut board with black lettering surrounded by a zinc frame, and with a bowl for flowers at the base, at the time it bore forty-eight names. Mounted on the wall of a shop at the bottom of Smith Street and the top of the High Street, it was unveiled in the presence of the then Lieutenant-Governor, General Sir Reginald Hart VC, KCB, KCVO. By June the following year it was realised that the Shrine could no longer accommodate an ever-expanding list of names, and so was enlarged to form a triptych, the new version being dedicated in February 1920.

◦ The restored First World War Street Shrine that can be seen in St Pauls Church in Brighton. The names are handwritten on paper. (Courtesy of Robert Mitchell)

By 1955, the Shrine had suffered, like so many others, from the ravages of time and nature. Consequently, when the building on which it was positioned was due for refurbishment, the Shrine was removed. Having been long superseded by the main Bailiwick War Memorial, the decision was taken not to replace it.

It was not only the elements that led to the gradual loss of Street Shrines. On 9 January 1922, Thomas William Stalberg, a 36-year-old Seaman, was fined 40s. at West Ham Police Court for being drunk and disorderly and 'wilfully damaging a war shrine in Edward-street'. It was stated that 'the prisoner tore down the shrine, which was fixed to the wall of one of the houses, and threw it in the gutter. It bore the names of the men living in Edward-street who served in the war.' Stalberg's name was one of those on the Shrine.

With the Armistice in 1918, and the knowledge that subject to the signing of an official treaty the fighting was at an end, the nation looked to more permanent forms of commemoration. From the smallest hamlets and villages, to the largest towns and cities, communities turned to the more conventional forms of War Memorial that still sit at the centre of the nation's Remembrance to this day.

REMEMBERING THE FALLEN 27

REMEMBERING THE FALLEN 1914-1918 THE IMPERIAL WAR GRAVES COMMISSION

THE IMPERIAL WAR GRAVES COMMISSION

There had never been any official system of recording the graves of servicemen killed or missing in action but thanks to the persistence of one man, an enormous scheme was devised to ensure that those who lost their lives in conflict would never be forgotten.

◐ A visitor to Gouzeaucourt New British Cemetery (located ten miles south west of Cambrai) searching for the grave of one of the fallen. The wooden cross in the foreground denotes the last resting place of Lance Corporal B.S. Allen, 2nd Battalion Lincolnshire Regiment, who was killed on 2 April 1917. (Historic Military Press)

THE IMPERIAL WAR GRAVES COMMISSION REMEMBERING THE FALLEN 1914-1918

Ever since 1887, there had been periodic meetings between government leaders from the self-governing colonies and dominions of the British Empire. These were originally termed 'Colonial Conferences' and after 1907, 'Imperial Conferences'. Before the outbreak of war in 1914 the last Imperial Conference had been in 1911. The need for a combined approach to the conflict across the Empire led to the decision not only to reinstate the Imperial Conferences, but to hold an Imperial War Conference at the same time whilst all the Imperial leaders were together.

As a result, on 21 March 1917, the first Imperial Conference of the war, and the concurrent first ever Imperial War Conference, was held in London. The leaders of Canada, Australia, South Africa, New Zealand, Newfoundland and India met to discuss the war effort. This included, for the first time, a non-White representative in the form of General Maharaja Sir Ganga Singh. Though the first War Conference continued until 27 April 1917, it was on the eighth day, Friday, 13 April 1917, that the heads of state from the self-governing dominions, meeting at the Colonial Office in London, agreed to consider the method by which the remains of those that had died during the war should be treated.

○ A photograph taken at No.10 Downing Street during the first ever Imperial War Conference. David Lloyd George can be seen in the centre of the front row, whilst General Maharaja Sir Ganga Singh is in the centre row, second from the left. (US Library of Congress)

The only existing organisation at that time was the Directorate of Graves Registration and Enquiries, as the Graves Registration Commission had come to be known, which, as we have already seen, was led by Brigadier, later Major General, Fabian Ware.

Under the heading, 'Care of Soldiers' Graves', it was noted that a draft charter had already been prepared by Ware for the Prince of Wales' Committee for the Care of Soldiers Graves. In this, it was stated that because of the very sensitive nature of the subject, the interests of the deceased and their relatives would be best served by the formation of a new organisation, rather than the work being entrusted to an existing body.

○ The original wooden grave marker for seven members of the 2nd/1st East Anglian Field Ambulance, Royal Army Medical Corps, killed in action 20 July 1917. A handwritten comment on the rear states that the seven were killed by 'one shell'. They are all buried in Gaza War Cemetery. (Historic Military Press)

IN SOME FOREIGN FIELD

The situation was compounded by the fact that Ware's existing organisation was heavily burdened and the fact that the tens of thousands of graves of British servicemen were, of course, on foreign soil, over which Britain had no jurisdiction. General Macready, therefore, suggested that Ware should ask the French Government if the UK could purchase the land where the cemeteries were found. The French, very generously, offered such land for free in perpetuity and even said that they would take responsibility for maintaining the cemeteries. The offer of the land was warmly welcomed, but it was decided that Britain should look after the graves of its own men. Working together, the French authorities and Ware's team, the ground was carefully selected so as to cause as little disruption to the area's agriculture, and cemeteries began to take on a uniform pattern. Each grave, the French insisted, had to be nine to twelve inches apart and the path between the rows of graves was not to exceed three feet.

The work of the Graves Registration Commission was already prompting many people in the UK to write asking for details of their lost relatives and even for photographs of the graves. It was not the duty of the Commission to pass on such information to next of kin, but Ware decided that he would try to meet such requests. The additional cost of providing photographs was also funded by the Red Cross. Before the end of 1915, thousands of photographs of graves had been taken in response to requests, and prints sent to the next of kin along with details of where the grave was to be found and, if the grave was in a cemetery, which was the nearest train station for those who might want to visit the graves after the war. ➡

REMEMBERING THE FALLEN **29**

REMEMBERING THE FALLEN 1914-1918 THE IMPERIAL WAR GRAVES COMMISSION

A number of war graves pictured in Jerusalem War Cemetery in the years after the Armistice. Jerusalem War Cemetery is three miles north of the walled city and is situated on the neck of land at the north end of the Mount of Olives, to the west of Mount Scopus. The large grave marker is that of Nursing Sister Charlotte Berrie, Queen Alexandria's Imperial Military Nursing Service, who died on 8 January 1919 aged 32. She was the sister of Mrs Gladys M. Macgrega of 12, Brightmore Street, Neutral Bay, Sydney, NSW, Australia. (US Library of Congress)

Government's Office of Works argued that it should be its responsibility to look after the cemeteries. But to maintain what would eventually be tens of thousands of graves in hundreds of cemeteries in Italy, Macedonia, the Balkans, the Greek islands, Egypt, East Africa, Iraq and even as far afield as India and China, as well as the Western Front and the UK, was an enormous undertaking and Ware and Macready both felt that a separate body dedicated solely to the upkeep of the graves and cemeteries was what was needed. It was also pointed out that the dead were not just from Britain but included many men from across the Empire and to leave the maintenance to a British department would be inappropriate.

IMPERIAL WAR GRAVES COMMISSION

So it was, that the meetings of the Imperial Heads of State in April 1917 offered Ware the chance to put his ideas forward in his draft charter: 'It was felt that the nation would expect the Government should undertake the care of the last resting places of those who had fallen,' Ware explained in the pre-amble to the charter. He pointed out that if proper provision was made for the dead then the country and the Empire, 'would be spared the reflections which weighed on the conscience of the British nation when, nearly twenty years after the conclusion of the Crimean War, it became known that the last resting places of those who had fallen in the war, except in individual instances, remained uncared for and neglected'.

In early 1916, before the cataclysmic Battle of the Somme, the Commission had become the Directorate of Graves Registration and Enquiries and Ware became a brigadier. The Directorate's responsibilities were also extended to other theatres of war, with units being set up in Salonika, Greece, Egypt and Mesopotamia. As it was then certain that the cemeteries would be permanent structures, Ware considered their layout, developing a horticultural policy under a new National Committee for the Care of Soldiers' Graves which also sought advice from the assistant director of Kew Gardens. By the end of May 1916, Ware had identified the sites for around 200 permanent cemeteries.

What was still lacking, though, was a method of maintaining these cemeteries after the war. All that the Directorate was charged with was the registering of graves and the establishment of the cemeteries. At first the British

ENGLISH HERITAGE
Sir
FABIAN WARE
1869-1949
Founder of the
Imperial War Graves
Commission
lived here
1911-1919

The blue plaque marking Fabian Ware's residence at 14 Wyndham Place, Marylebone.

British and German sailors buried side by side in Frederikshavn Cemetery. Pictured after the Armistice, in a photograph believed to have been taken during the 1920s, the British memorial is on the left; the German one nearest the camera. Frederikshavn is a port in northern Jutland, about twenty-five miles from the northernmost point of Denmark. Buried there are four First World War casualties, all naval ratings killed in the Battle of Jutland. (Historic Military Press)

30 REMEMBERING THE FALLEN

THE IMPERIAL WAR GRAVES COMMISSION   REMEMBERING THE FALLEN 1914-1918

The French Government had, of course, granted the land for the cemeteries for free and it was expected that, once the Germans had been evicted from Belgium, that the Belgian Government would offer the same provision in its country, likewise in the other theatres around the world. The only thing that was needed, Ware explained to the Heads of State, was a body to oversee the maintenance of the cemeteries.

This organisation, Ware suggested, could be founded by voluntary contributions from the Dominions and the UK, and partly by private donations. This, though, seemed an unsatisfactory way of treating those who had made the ultimate sacrifice. A far better idea, Ware went on to propose, was 'to create a permanent statutory organisation … If this second course were adopted, an Act of the Imperial Parliament would probably be necessary to establish a Fund and to authorize gifts to that Fund. Similar Acts might have to be passed by the Dominion Parliaments. Commissioners would then be approved by Royal Warrant.'

With the number of registered graves already reaching more than 150,000, to allay any fears that this organisation might cost too much to the countries already

○ Work on the laying out and construction of Hooge Crater Cemetery, which is just off the Menin Road a couple of miles east of Ypres, is pictured underway at the end of, or just after, the First World War. Note the wooden duckboards and original IWGC grave markers. Today there are 5,916 Commonwealth servicemen of the First World War buried or commemorated in this cemetery. Of this number, 3,570 are unidentified, but special memorials record the names of a number of casualties either known or believed to be buried among them, or whose graves in other cemeteries were destroyed by shell fire. The cemetery was designed by Sir Edwin Lutyens. (Historic Military Press)

○ In an effort to explain its work and policies, in 1919 the HMSO, on behalf of the Imperial War Graves Commission, published this 16-page booklet. The text was written by Rudyard Kipling. (Historic Military Press)

impoverished by war, Ware wrote: 'The staff required at the outset to complete the work of registration and to organise the burial grounds would be gradually reduced, until it was only of such dimensions as were required to supervise the maintenance of the cemeteries and to administer such funds as were necessary for the ceremonial visits which would be paid periodically to the cemeteries abroad and by which the memory of the dead would be honoured and the common sacrifices of the Allies would be recalled.'

Ware then pointed to the growing demand for suitable, official, recognition of the dead: 'The question of permanent memorials, whether of a collective or individual character, the erection of which at present is forbidden owing to military necessities, is so greatly agitating the public mind that there should be no more delay than is inevitable in satisfying public feeling on the question. Isolated appeals for funds in this connection from private individuals or dependent committees have already begun to appear in the newspapers.'

In conclusion, Ware wrote: 'If the Government of the United Kingdom, of the Dominions and of India are of opinion that the moral contingencies involved in the inadequate treatment of the graves of those who have fallen demand at least as much attention as the material result of the War, they will undoubtedly consider … the matter.'

Such an appeal could not be ignored by the Imperial heads of state and Ware's proposal was accepted. The result was that on 21 May 1917, the Imperial War Graves Commission was established by Royal Charter, with the Prince of Wales serving as President and Ware as Vice-Chairman. Its remit was to care for the remains of all members of the armed forces of the British Empire who 'died from wounds inflicted, accident occurring, or disease contracted, while on active service whether on land or sea'. The IWGC was charged with providing burials, the erection and maintenance of memorials and the recording and registration of the graves – including those graves that lay outside cemeteries.

As any visitor to a cemetery of what is today the Commonwealth War Graves Commission knows, the cemeteries are similar in design, though each is unique in structure. Following its formation, the IWGC selected three of the most eminent architects of the day - Sir Edwin ➡

○ A view of Hooge Crater Cemetery today. (R.J.M. Bishop/Shutterstock)

REMEMBERING THE FALLEN 31

REMEMBERING THE FALLEN 1914-1918 THE IMPERIAL WAR GRAVES COMMISSION

Lutyens, Sir Herbert Baker and Sir Reginald Blomfield - to begin the work of designing and constructing the many cemeteries and memorials. Rudyard Kipling was tasked as literary advisor to recommend inscriptions.

Ware also asked Sir Frederic Kenyon, Director of the British Museum, to interpret the differing approaches of these three principal architects. The report he presented to the Commission in November 1918, emphasised equality as the core ideology:

'The [Imperial War Graves] Commission has already laid down one principle, which goes far towards determining the disposition of the cemeteries; the principle, namely, of equality of treatment ... As soon as the question was faced, it was felt that the

○ Tyne Cot Cemetery at Zonnebeke as it would have appeared at the end of the war, or just after. Note the German pillbox in the background – this can still be seen in the cemetery today. (Historic Military Press)

○ King George V and Sir Fabian Ware, on the left holding the papers, with other officers and dignitaries pictured during a visit to Tyne Cot Cemetery, Belgium, in the years after the formation of the Imperial War Graves Commission. The men in the image are, from left to right, Major W.B. Binnie, IWGC Director of Works; Captain John Truelove, Architect; Major General Fabian Ware, Director General IWGC; Colonel Clive Wigram, the King's Private Secretary; Field Marshal Douglas Haig; Colonel H. Goodland, Deputy Controller of the IWGC; the King; and T. Elvidge, Head Gardener at Tyne Cot.

provision of monuments could not be left to individual initiative. In a few cases, where money and good taste were not wanting, a satisfactory result would be obtained, in the sense that a fine individual monument would be erected. In the large majority of cases either no monument would be erected, or it would be poor in quality; and the total result would be one of inequality, haphazard and disorder. The cemetery would become a collection of individual memorials, a few good, but many bad, and with a total want of congruity and uniformity. The monuments of the more well-to-do would overshadow those of their poorer comrades; the whole sense of comradeship and of common service would be lost.

'The Commission, on the other hand, felt that where the sacrifice had been common, the memorial should be common also; and they desired that the cemeteries should be the symbol of a great Army and a united Empire. It was therefore ordained that what was done for one should be done for all, and that all, whatever their military rank or position in civil life, should have equal treatment in their graves.'

Such a policy, however, was not universally welcomed at the time, as Kenyon himself went on to note in his report: 'It is necessary to face the fact that this decision has given pain in some quarters, and pain which the Commissioners would have been glad to avoid. Not a few relatives have been looking forward to placing a memorial of their own choosing over the graves which mean so much to them; some have devoted much time and thought to making such a memorial beautiful and significant. Yet it is hoped that even these will realize that they are asked to join in an action of even higher significance. The sacrifice of the individual is a great idea and worthy of commemoration; but the community of sacrifice, the service of a common cause, the comradeship of arms which has brought together men of all ranks and grades – these are greater ideas, which should be commemorated in those cemeteries where they lie together, the representatives of their country in the lands in which they served.' It was through words such as this that Kenyon's report outlined the principles by which the organisation still operates over a century later.

As an honorary artistic advisor to the IWGC, Kenyon also wrote: 'The general appearance of a British cemetery will be that of an enclosure with plots of grass or flowers (or both) separated by paths of varying size, and set with orderly rows of headstones, uniform in height and width ... and at some prominent spot will rise the Cross, as the symbol ... of the self-sacrifice of the men who now lie beneath its shadow.'

Kenyon's vision became reality and the many beautiful cemeteries found around the world rose in stark splendour from the scarred battlefields of the Great War to become the destination of many pilgrims and visitors after the war, just as they still are today. ●

○ Tyne Cot Cemetery and Tyne Cot Memorial are located a few miles to the north of Ypres. 'Tyne Cot' or 'Tyne Cottage' was the name given by the Northumberland Fusiliers to a barn which stood near the level crossing on the Passchendaele-Broodseinde road. It is now the largest Commonwealth war cemetery in the world in terms of burials. (Shutterstock)

32 REMEMBERING THE FALLEN

NEW 2019 BROCHURE OUT NOW!

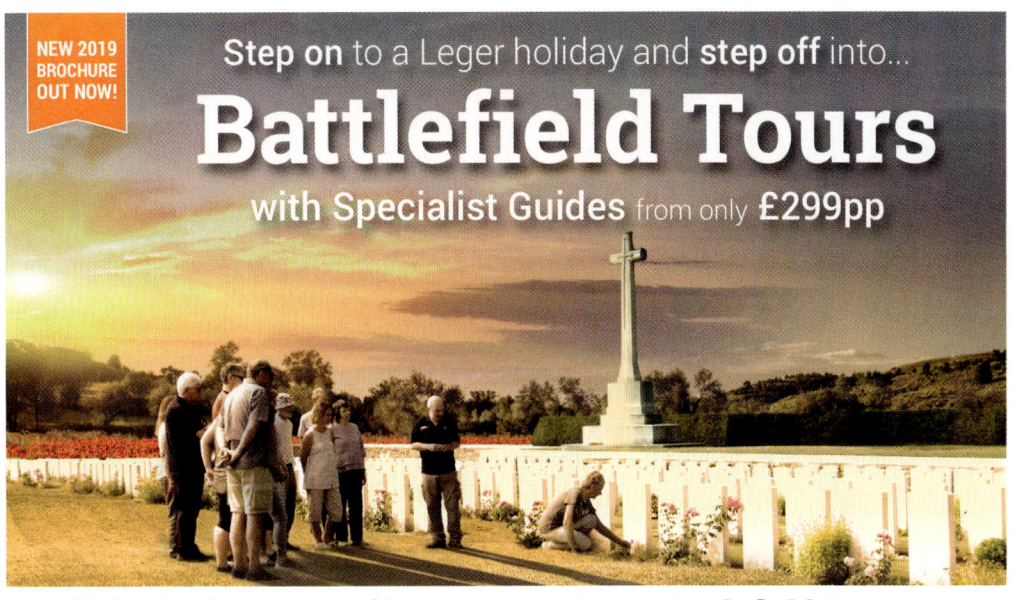

Step on to a Leger holiday and **step off** into...

Battlefield Tours

with **Specialist Guides** from only **£299pp**

leger HOLIDAYS

Over 75 escorted tours to choose from including WW1, WW2 and other conflicts.

WW1 – All Quiet on the Western Front
4 days from only £299

WW1 – Beer & Battlefields
5 days from only £599

WW2 – D-Day Landings in Normandy
4 days from only £299

Walk in the footsteps of heroes® on a Leger Battlefield Tour.

Thanks to our expert **Specialist Guides**, who accompany every tour, you'll embark on a fascinating journey of Remembrance and discovery.

Taking in a combination of battlefields, memorials and War Cemeteries you'll learn why battles were fought at particular locations and your guide will help you interpret the landscape and look for signs of the battle evident today.

All coach tours feature FREE **local joining points across the UK**, and the option to upgrade to **Silver Service coach** with extra legroom and rear lounge, or **Luxuria**, with extra wide seats and touch screen TVs.

Call or visit our website today for a brochure!
01709 786 639 • **www.legerbattlefields.co.uk**

ABTA No. V3582

017342

WORLD WAR I CENTENARY

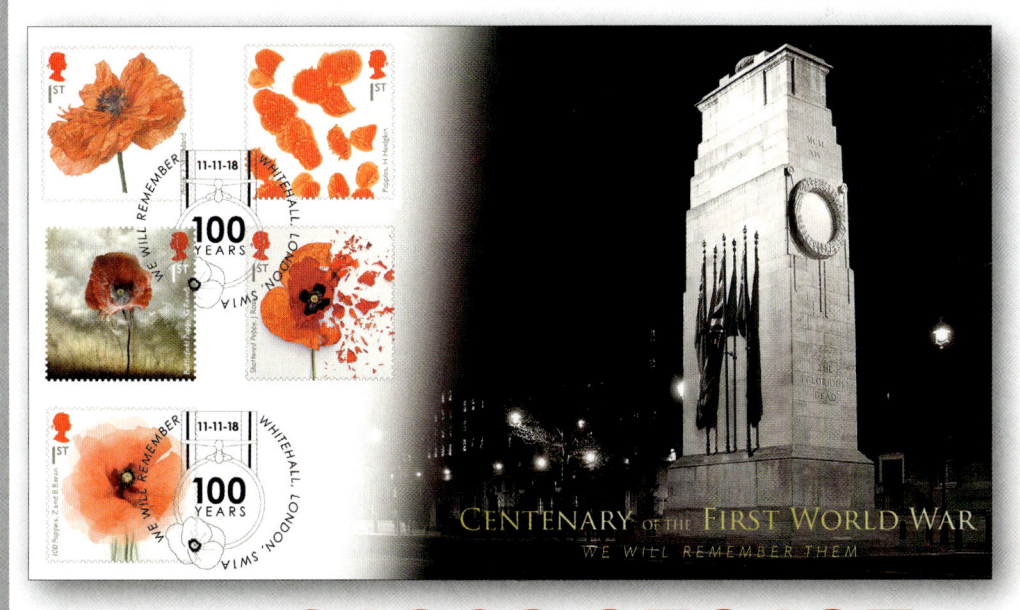

LIMITED EDITION GREAT WAR STAMPS COLLECTABLE FEATURING:

• Five poppy stamps - one issued in each WWI centenary year (2014-2018)

• We Will Remember postmark 11/11/2018

BCSP56
£18.50
plus £2.45 p&p

Call us on **01303 278137** or order online at
www.buckinghamcovers.com/fallen1918

Buckingham Covers are world experts in limited edition stamp collectables, holding a fantastic array of collectable covers and autographs across a broad range of subjects. This is just one of our recent issues. If you like what you see visit our website to see more!

Buckingham Covers, Warren House, Shearway Road, Folkestone, Kent CT19 4BF   email: betty@buckinghamcovers.com

Please allow up to 28 days for delivery after issue date (11th November 2018)

REMEMBERING THE FALLEN 1914-1918 FINISHING THE TASK

FINISHING THE TASK

It was after the Armistice that the work of the Imperial War Graves Commission really began in earnest. With the land for cemeteries and memorials guaranteed, it was then that the enormous task of recording the details of the dead began in earnest.

When the fighting in the First World War came to an end in November 1918 barely half of the Western Front's dead had been given a proper burial in a designated military cemetery. The battlefields were still strewn with hundreds of hastily made 'soldiers' cemeteries, some little more than clusters of graves in fields, by roadsides or canal banks. There were thousands of isolated graves in the battle area and countless bodies still lay out, unburied, in what had been No Man's Land.

'Post-war clearance of the battlefields began in earnest early in 1919,' notes a Commonwealth War Graves Commission account, 'when the old battlefields were swept and swept again for small cemeteries (of less than forty graves), battlefield graves and the previously unburied dead. All of those found were gathered into 'concentration' cemeteries, either newly created or built up around already established burial grounds.

'Battlefield exhumation and reburial was undertaken by special Graves Concentration Units. Initially, these were made up of volunteers from infantry and labour units but later a scheme of direct recruitment into the Labour Corps for a limited period of service was introduced. Not surprisingly, such duties attracted extra pay. Living and working conditions for the exhumation squads were difficult to say the least, the work mostly being undertaken in a battlefield's "devastated area" – a cratered, desolate landscape covered in

1 The captions to the images in this article are included in the main text from page 38.
(All images courtesy of the Commonwealth War Graves Commission)

FINISHING THE TASK **REMEMBERING THE FALLEN 1914-1918**

rank vegetation, which was waterlogged through poor weather and shattered drainage systems, and where the men faced additional hazards from rusting battlefield debris and unexploded ordnance.'

The work itself was deeply unpleasant – the bodies they found were still in a state of decomposition yet required close examination to find means of identification. Private John McCauley, a member of an exhumation company, recalled that, 'For the first week or two I could scarcely endure the experience we met with, but I gradually became hardened.'

Speed was of the essence, too, both for sanitary reasons and to keep pace with reconstruction work being undertaken by the French and Belgian populations keen to return to their homes and lives. Special 'Flying Squads' had to be ready to rush to areas not yet swept by the exhumation parties if bodies were found during building or cultivation work.

Despite these pressures, the exhumation squads were methodical and meticulous in their searches and, with most of the men having seen active service themselves, were painstaking in their search for anything that would help identify a fallen comrade.

AN 'APPALLING TASK'

On 29 December 1919, *The Scotsman* published an article written by 'an ex-Staff Officer' who helped explain the situation regarding the burial of the dead at that stage: 'There are two quite distinct authorities concerned in the work – (1) The Directorate of Graves Registration and Enquiries, which is a military organisation staffed and manned entirely by soldiers, responsible, like any other military

REMEMBERING THE FALLEN 1914-1918 FINISHING THE TASK

3

4

Department through the General Officer Commanding in France and Flanders to the War Office; (2) the Imperial War Graves Commission, which is financed by the Treasury and is responsible for the war graves on all the battle fronts ...

'The duty of the Directorate is to complete the work which was done, so far as was humanly possible, during hostilities by comrades of the fallen – i.e., to bury the body (in a cemetery if possible, if not on the battlefield), to register the grave in as permanent a form as possible, to report the exact position of the grave, and to take such steps as they could to secure the cemetery or grave from molestation till permanent memorials could be erected.

'The duty of the [Imperial War Graves] Commission is the construction of permanent memorials in stone and the transformation of the simple, perishable cemetery, with wooden crosses and barbed-wire fences, into a properly-walled enclosure, with the great stone cross, the stone of memorial, and separate headstones. The Directorate is, therefore, now engaged on completing the vast and onerous task which could not be finished when we were fighting, and on handing over to the Commission each cemetery as it is completed, with full documentary evidence and all available data as to identification and individual particulars.

'A further task, which a year ago would have seemed impossible and in many ways undesirable in itself, was imposed upon the Directorate by the decision, arrived at after discussion between the Governments concerned, that, normally, a cemetery to be preserved permanently must consist of not less than fifty graves, and that all smaller cemeteries and isolated graves (the latter numbering about 200,000) must be concentrated into new cemeteries or extensions of existing cemeteries (military or communal).

'To perform this appalling task the Directorate was given the services of approximately 18,000 soldiers, including (temporarily) about 1,000 Australians (who worked near Villers-Bretonneux) and 1,000 Canadians (who worked along the Bapaume-Albert road and on the famous field of Vimy Ridge). British troops, as above stated, had, with a little help from French and Portuguese detachments, to clear the whole area lying north of a line drawn roughly through Amiens, Villers-Bretonneux, Péronne, Le Cateau and Namur, up to the sea. They had also to furnish detachments to work with French troops in connection with British graves in the whole of the war area south of this line.

'The magnitude of the task, to anyone who seriously considers the conditions – including the problems of administering and accommodating troops in the desolated area, with all the old means of communication reduced almost to nothing in the natural process of economy, and with inhabitants everywhere eager to resume possession of such supplies and accommodation as remained – will need no further emphasis.'

The same ex-Staff Officer went on to explain just why the policy of concentrating many of the graves was necessary: 'Its purpose is obviously twofold – (1) to prevent the gradual disappearance of such graves as were threatened with obliteration through the impossibility of guaranteeing their upkeep, and the inevitable callousness in time to come of

5

FINISHING THE TASK REMEMBERING THE FALLEN 1914-1918

farmers and manufacturers; (2) to limit as far as possible the loss imposed upon agriculturists and others by the reservation of countless parcels of land, selected under stress of war without regard to ownership or the proximity of houses, factories, water supply, railways , &c .

'Practically every soldier to whom I have spoken would have favoured the transfer of the crosses only, in preference to the exhumation and concentration of actual remains, but a reverent consideration for bereaved relatives rendered such a course unthinkable. Those who, most naturally, are horrified by the idea of exhumation must realise that to leave graves in the middle of inaccessible areas, deep in shell holes, in the ruins of houses, in the surface of country roads which reconstruction must reopen for traffic, on the banks of streams and reservoirs, on railway embankments, in ruined woods under overturned tree trunks, in the sodden marsh-land round Ypres, Zillibeke, Nieuport, Péronne, was at least equally unthinkable. Many have already been lost in places like these, and in course of time all must have ultimately disappeared. The consideration shown by many a French farmer this year in respecting graves located here and there in his cornfields cannot be expected to last for ever or to weigh equally with his successors ...

'The terrible work of exhumation is done with all possible reverence, difficult though it necessarily is to mitigate the horrors of it. Chaplains are present wherever it is possible to secure the attendance of the few who are still in France, and the remains are removed under the Union Jack and reinterred with all possible care. And the work has one most important and valuable side – namely, that in a surprisingly large number of cases bodies buried in the heat of battle as "Unknown", or by the Germans with wrong names and particulars, are identified by some document or possession which has resisted decay. During some periods of work the percentage of such identifications has reached as high a figure as 80. Apart from exhumation, relatives would never have known where the body rested. In one case a German cross, "To an Unknown Englishman", was found to cover 42 remains, of which 37 were identified!

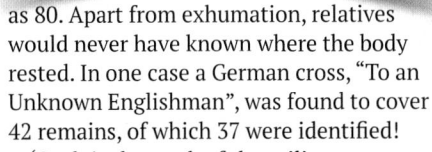

'Such is the work of the military directorate. He who would make light of its difficulties or throw doubt upon the spirit in which they are confronted would do a grave injustice to a number of soldiers whose reverent determination to make a success is based upon real knowledge of the conditions under which their comrades died.'

The achievements of the various Graves Concentration Units is evidenced by the following report which was published in the *Aberdeen Press and Journal* on Wednesday, 22 October 1919: 'The work of identifying the solitary and in many cases unmarked graves of the British soldiers who fell in action in France and Flanders and of concentrating these graves in cemeteries near the reserved battlefields has now proceeded so far that the G.O.C. and the Director of Graves Registration in

REMEMBERING THE FALLEN 37

REMEMBERING THE FALLEN 1914-1918 FINISHING THE TASK

9

France hope to bring it to end in March next. By the beginning of last June 22,000 graves had been concentrated, and this number has steadily increased till it now stands at 128,000. The exhumations and concentrations during the past months have averaged 8,000 per week. Many of the bodies recovered from unmarked graves and shell holes have been those of men who have been reported as missing.'

By the time the Graves Concentration Units were disbanded in the spring of 1920, tens of thousands of bodies had been recovered and reburied, but bodies continued to be discovered in numbers for years after. Even today, the remains of as many as twenty or thirty First World War soldiers can be found on the old Western Front each year.

A GRAVES CONCENTRATION UNIT AT WORK

Captain G. Crawford, who commanded 68 Labour Company, was one of the first engaged on exhumation and reburial work. He drew up a set of working instructions which became the standard operating procedure for Graves Concentration Units.

10

Sections of Crawford's graphic text follow. They help explain the set of photographs which, supplied courtesy of the Commonwealth War Graves Commission, accompanies this article. These images chart the men of 129 Labour Company at work on the Passchendaele battlefield, near Ypres, in 1919. The bodies they found were taken to Passchendaele New British Cemetery, a concentration cemetery of more than 2,000 burials. More than three-quarters of the men buried there are unidentified.

The photographer was Corporal Ivan Bawtree. During the war, Bawtree initially worked as a photographer with the British Red Cross attached to a Graves Registration Unit on the Western Front. He later transferred to the Imperial War Graves Commission. Bawtree's job involved taking photographs of grave markers for the Directorate of Graves Registration and Enquiries to forward to relatives of the dead, but he also created many other images which give us a unique view of life in the military zone both during and immediately after the war.

11

PICTURES 1 and 2

'Each squad [of 32 men] should be given an area consisting of a map square of 500 yards, which must be thoroughly searched and cleared … advantage should be taken of natural features where possible, as it is much easier to search the area, say, between a road and a trench, or a line of pill boxes, than to work upon imaginary lines between flags … the men, should be posted in extended order at intervals of about six yards. They must advance slowly, searching the area thoroughly, and avoid bunching. Wherever a body is found, a stake is to be planted.'

THE FALLEN 1914-1918

often have to be traversed. Motor ambulances are used where parties are working near the main road, or to take the bodies from the wagons as soon as they reach the main road ... each GS wagon can take five loaded stretchers, four on top and one in the bottom. A stretcher should be allotted to each body, except in the case of fragmentary remains ...

'A spare man from the Exhumation Company should be allotted to each GS wagon to see that required stores are taken up to the working parties. He should walk behind the wagon when it is loaded with bodies to see that no accident happens on the way to the cemetery.'

PICTURE 3
'Experience only teaches men where bodies will probably be found in graves which are not visible, but the following signs are characteristic ... rifles or posts bearing helmets or equipment, placed at the head of graves ... remains or equipment upon the surface or protruding from the ground ... rat holes – these sometimes will show small bones or pieces of equipment brought to the surface by the rats ... discolouration of grass, earth or water – grass is often of a vivid bluish green colour where bodies are buried and water turns a greenish black or grey... The area having been thoroughly searched and staked out, the work of exhumation begins.'

PICTURE 4
'Each party of four should have with them shovels, rubber gloves, canvas and rope, Cresol [disinfectant] and stretchers ... at the present time, conditions are against rapid work: the battlefields are covered with a growth of rank grass and nettles, in places almost waist high, which often conceals the more obscure traces by which bodies can be discovered ... an area must be swept and re-swept before it is definitely decided that no graves have been overlooked. This is especially important because after an area has been described as clear, any graves registered in that area which have not been found [must] definitely be regarded as lost.'

PICTURE 5
'It has been found advisable to impress upon [the men] that ... the work is of vital importance, having regard to the number of men still missing, many of whom can be found and identified if the work is carefully done ... the greater the stress laid upon the need for identification, the greater the interest the men take in the work.'

'In the actual work of exhumation, the men should be warned not to dig too closely to the bodies, but well outside them. Such a precaution renders the work easier, prevents disturbance of the bodies and, most important of all, reveals whether more than one man is buried in one particular spot ... men engaged upon exhumation should be instructed to use Cresol generously, especially for washing their hands and their gloves after handling bodies or effects ... during the summer, work should be in the early morning.'

PICTURE 6
'The body, having been exhumed, is placed upon the canvas and a careful search is made for any effects which may lead to identification. The pockets should be searched, and a special examination made of the neck, wrists and braces, where identity discs may be found.

'All effects are placed in a ration bag and sent to the cemetery attached to the body...where more than one body is found the remains must be kept and sent to the cemetery together, and the labels so marked that the cemetery officer will bury them side by side ... it is often possible from records to identify unknowns from the fact that they are known to have been buried with the identified men ...

'The remains are then wrapped in the canvas, which is tied up and labelled ... It has been found useful to mark all labels of one group of bodies with a distinctive letter of the alphabet, followed by a number showing the order in which they are to be buried ... a union flag should be provided for each wagon or ambulance to cover the bodies.'

PICTURE 7
'The work of transporting the bodies to the cemetery is usually carried out by GS [General Service] wagons. No other transport can be used over the rough tracks which

PICTURE 8
'The bodies being brought to the cemetery, all effects are examined carefully and compared with the labels attached. A magnifying glass should be used to read the discs ... if any query arises as a result of the examination, the exhuming officer, whose signature will be on the label, can be questioned when he reports at the cemetery, as he should do each day.'

PICTURES 9, 10 and 11
'The size of the digging party depends upon the number of bodies expected to be received at the cemetery each day ... under ordinary conditions, ten to twelve men should be able to dig a trench sufficient to take twenty bodies, and to carry out the reburials during ordinary working hours. It is the sanitary man's duty to see that as soon as the bodies have been removed, the stretchers are washed in Cresol and returned to the wagons.'

PICTURES 12 and 13
'The bodies are then placed in their respective positions and the graves filled in either with or without a committal service (this will depend on whether, in the opinion of the Officer present at the exhumation, the body has previously been properly committed or not) ... stakes bearing labels giving particulars of the men buried beneath are then erected at the head of the graves ... until the GRUs [Graves Registration Units] erect crosses.'

REMEMBERING THE FALLEN 1914-1918 THE CENOTAPH

THE CENOTAPH

In 1920 the Cenotaph was unveiled as the United Kingdom's official National War Memorial.

The concept of the Cenotaph arose from the perceived need to remember the dead of the war during the Victory Parade (also called the Peace Day Parade) on 19 July 1919. It marked the formal end of the First World War that had taken place with the signing of the Treaty of Versailles four weeks earlier on 28 June. Sir Edwin Lutyens was given two weeks to design a non-denominational shrine made out of wood and plaster. It was Lutyens who suggested this structure be named the Cenotaph, a word derived from the Greek for 'empty tomb'.

As one account states, Lutyens' temporary design 'had the same shape as the later permanent stone structure and consisted of a pylon that rose in a series of set-backs to the empty tomb (cenotaph) on its summit. The wreaths at each end and on top were made from laurel rather than the later carved stone sculptures.' The siting of this first cenotaph on Whitehall was only confirmed two weeks before the 19 July parades; indeed, it was only unveiled on 18 July.

◯ **King George V unveiling the Cenotaph in Whitehall, London, on 11 November 1920** – note the Union Flag falling to the ground on the left. It was decided not to dedicate the memorial, as not all of the dead it commemorates are Christian. The ceremony was part of a larger procession in which the body of the Unknown Warrior was taken to Westminster Abbey. (Historic Military Press)

40 REMEMBERING THE FALLEN

THE CENOTAPH REMEMBERING THE FALLEN 1914-1918

○ The King laying a wreath at the base of the Cenotaph during its official unveiling on 11 November 1920. (Historic Military Press)

○ A picture of the Cenotaph in Whitehall after its official unveiling on 11 November 1920. The message bottom left states: 'From Commander in Chief Atlantic Fleet, Flag Captain, Officers and Ship's Company of HMS *Queen Elizabeth*.' (Historic Military Press)

○ Pictured in the hours and days after the Cenotaph's unveiling ceremony, members of the public gather around to read the inscriptions on the many wreaths. (Historic Military Press)

○ The Cenotaph in Whitehall, London, pictured after a Remembrance Day service during the 1930s. Crafted between 1919 and 1920 by Holland, Hannen & Cubitts, the Cenotaph is 35 feet tall and weighs 120 tonnes. (Historic Military Press)

It was the Cenotaph which most captured the public imagination during the victory celebrations on 19 July, and after the parade many of the bereaved laid wreaths at its base. It was evident that a more permanent monument was required. The words of one letter written to *The Times* on the day of the unveiling sums up how many felt: 'The Cenotaph in Whitehall is so simple and dignified that it would be a pity to consider it merely an ephemeral erection. It appears to be of more lasting material than the other decorative efforts, and I suggest that it should be retained either in its present form or rendered in granite or stone with bronze wreaths to take the place of the evergreens.'

As a substitute for a grave, the initial cenotaph was taken up by huge numbers of mourners, who laid flowers at its base in daunting quantities: over 1.25 million persons came to pay their respects in the first week after it was unveiled. Though it had only been intended that the structure would stand for a week, pressure to retain it in one form or another continued to mount. So much so, that on 30 July 1919, the War Cabinet announced that a permanent memorial should replace the wooden version. It would be designated as Britain's official national war memorial.

Despite this announcement, there were still those with questions or concerns. On 13 August 1919, for example, Lieutenant Colonel Nathan Raw, the MP for Liverpool Wavertree, asked the 'Commissioner of Works if he will consider the advisability of erecting the permanent memorial to "Our Glorious Dead" on a site in Parliament Square on account of the danger to the public in having such a memorial in a crowded and busy thoroughfare?' The answer, from Sir Alfred Mond, was that the memorial would remain where it was.

REMEMBERING THE FALLEN **41**

REMEMBERING THE FALLEN 1914-1918 THE CENOTAPH

○ Similar cenotaphs to that in Whitehall were erected throughout Britain and the rest of the world. This is the imposing Cenotaph, which is more correctly referred to as the National War Memorial, in London, Ontario. (Shutterstock)

○ The Cenotaph that stands between Statue Square and City Hall in the centre of Hong Kong. Unveiled on 24 May 1923, by the then Governor Sir Reginald Stubbs, it is an almost exact copy of the Cenotaph in Whitehall. At the time, it was actually on Hong Kong's waterfront.

○ A view of the dedication ceremony of the Cenotaph in Wellington, New Zealand, on 28 November 1929. As was the case in London, the first Auckland cenotaph was a temporary structure made of wood and plaster. A scaled-down replica of the cenotaph designed by Edward Lutyens in Whitehall, London, it was first erected in front of the Auckland Town Hall in time for Anzac Day in 1922. (Alexander Turnbull Library/National Library of New Zealand)

Finally, on 23 October 1919, it was announced that the replacement would be a 'replica exact in every detail in permanent material of the present temporary structure'. After the original was removed in January 1920, the new Portland stone memorial was completed and installed, ready to be unveiled by King George V on Armistice Day in the same year.

After the original cenotaph was removed, the wooden top was displayed in the Imperial War Museum, which was then located in Crystal Palace, where it became a focus for Remembrance activities at the museum during the 1920s. The rest of the initial structure was handed over to wounded ex-servicemen at St Dunstan's who turned the wood into bases for bronze souvenir models of the Cenotaph. These were sold to raise funds for St Dunstan's work in helping care for blinded veterans.

THE UNVEILING CEREMONY

Among the many present at Whitehall on 11 November 1920, was James Bone, the London editor of the *Manchester Guardian*. He later wrote this account of the unveiling:

'There was gathered … at the Cenotaph an assembly representative of the Empire … Behind the King stood the Princes and a gathering representing the statesmen of England and the Dominions as well as the Forces and all the Churches.

'The Cenotaph seemed taller than its model because of the great Union Jacks that veiled it. Sir Edwin Lutyens stood near it in another company of officials. The crowd filled every inch of the pavement, packed close and orderly like slates on a roof. So it was as far as the eye could see till the curtain of mist descended, a hundred yards on, and shut out the rest of the world from the ceremony at the Cenotaph.

○ The initial conception of the Canadian National War Memorial pictured on display in Hyde Park, London, in 1933. The design work was finished in July 1932 and the bronzes were, with the permission of King George V, put on display in Hyde Park within a mock-up of the granite arch and plinth. The bronzes were relocated to Ottawa in the summer of 1937. The completed memorial, known as the National War Memorial and titled 'The Response', was unveiled by the King on 21 May 1939. (Library and Archives Canada)

'The Assembly at the Cenotaph was now in exact formation, leaving a great open space. The Foot Guards at a certain distance began a beautiful swerve which took them to the west of the Cenotaph, which they passed and fell into position on the Abbey side.'

At this point the gun carriage bearing the coffin of the Unknown Warrior drew up near the Cenotaph. After the King had placed a wreath on the coffin, 'the King,' continued Bone, 'then turned south and, touching a mechanism on the road, unveiled the Cenotaph, the two great Union Jacks falling to the ground with a tiny cloud of dust, settling in two coloured masses at the base.

'The Cenotaph, its new Portland stone a pale lemon, rose before us naked and

42 REMEMBERING THE FALLEN

THE CENOTAPH REMEMBERING THE FALLEN 1914-1918

Veterans march past the Cenotaph during a Remembrance Sunday service. (MoD/Crown Copyright 2018)

beautiful, focusing the growing light that was coming through the mist, and by its sudden apparition drawing all the significance of the moment to itself. After that the great silence, when the last boom of Big Ben had ceased to quiver in the air. All were uncovered, standing with bent heads. There was no motion, even from the horses standing in the gun carriage … It was not complete silence, for there was a high, monotonous screaming from some boat on the river, like a far-away keening for the dead. The people stood frozen.'

THE GREAT PROCESSION

'At last, the King lifted his head, and motion returned to the crowd,' added Bone. 'A woman had fainted, and she was carried away on a stretcher … The Last Post was sounded, and the procession reformed … Thus the great procession began which lasted, with only a few pauses, all the day.

'The VCs marched together, naval captains, gunners of the RFA, sergeants and soldiers of foot regiments, side by side with field officers, men in ordinary civilian clothes – they filed past inconspicuously, except that everyone was looking for them. Detachments from all branches of the Air Service and from the Mercantile Marine passed along, and a body of gentlemen in plain clothes, wearing miniature medals, and many other parties about whom the crowd wished information …

'The organised bodies of ex-soldiers and ex-sailors handed over their wreaths as they passed, and soon the Cenotaph rose out of a wonderful garden. During a long pause while rails were being put up around the monument, an extraordinary sight was seen. A hundred policemen in their bulky coats suddenly appeared at a quick step, all carrying huge wreaths of flowers, sent for official placing. It was expressive of the emotional tension of the scene that no one wanted to smile at this sight.

'The official part of the ceremony over, the great crowds that had gathered then began their pilgrimage; but a more moving sight appeared in six green motor coaches filled with men in hospital blue. In one coach were men who had lost limbs. In another were blinded soldiers; in another, soldiers with terrible injuries who could not rise like the others in their coaches as they came to the Cenotaph. Some of them must have envied their comrade who was to be buried in Westminster Abbey; some of them must have envied anyone who is dead. Men without legs, in hospital blues, passed along working their hand tricycles.'

THE NATION'S MEMORIAL

In his series *A Popular History of the Great War*, the renowned author and historian Sir J.A. Hammerton would later describe why the Cenotaph immediately began an integral part of the nation's Remembrance: 'If the Cenotaph had been ugly or dull in its design it would still hold the first place in the affections of the British people, for it is a permanent copy of the monument saluted by detachments of the Allied armies at the peace celebrations in 1919. But it is impossible that it should be dull or ugly, for the simple reason that if it had not at first given the deepest satisfaction to all who saw it, this monument would never have been duplicated in stone.'

Hammerton also wrote that, 'By common consent of the English [sic] people the most important individual killed in the Great War was not a leader so conspicuous even as Lord Kitchener; it was the average man, whose body is laid in the Unknown Warrior's grave in Westminster Abbey … The Unknown Warrior's grave commemorates the average of the men who died; the Cenotaph in Whitehall commemorates the whole of those men.'

Wreaths being laid at the Cenotaph, by Members of Parliament, during the Remembrance Sunday service in 2010. (MoD/Crown Copyright 2010)

REMEMBERING THE FALLEN 1914-1918 WAR MEMORIALS

WAR MEMORIALS

When it was known that the bodies of the dead would not be repatriated, efforts began to commemorate the fallen in cities, towns and villages across the land.

The great monuments at Vimy, Thiepval and Ypres and other notable battlefields of the First World War, stand as awe-inspiring tributes to the sacrifices of the armies of the Allied nations. But these are in distant lands, beyond the reach, and the pocket, of many, and represent the loss of men from widely geographical origins. Yet, more than anything, the war touched the lives of individuals and their communities at a very personal level. The stories of almost all the young men from a single street being killed, of workmates and football teams being decimated, were widespread. It was natural, therefore, that at a local level there was an unquenchable demand for memorials to be raised to commemorate those from the community who had lost their lives.

Possibly the most remarkable aspect of the tens of thousands of war memorials that can be seen across Britain and abroad, is their unique nature. While many are similar in design, few are the same. Certainly, it is the case that of all the war memorials set up by the cities and large towns not one of them is exactly like another. Part of the reason for this was not merely the ingenuity of the designers, but cost and practicality. In Ipswich, for example, the practical part of the war memorial was a new wing that was added to the East Suffolk and Ipswich Hospital. Likewise, a third of the memorial scheme in Colchester consisted of a block at the Essex County Hospital. In Norwich, the monument cost only £3,000, yet a total of between £150,000 and £160,000 was raised, so the balance was handed to the city's hospitals.

◉ The war memorial in the village of Inchbrook in Gloucestershire. Located in a small memorial garden beside the A46 Bath Road, it was dedicated in 1917. It is believed to have been the first village or community Great War memorial to be unveiled or dedicated in the UK. (Historic Military Press)

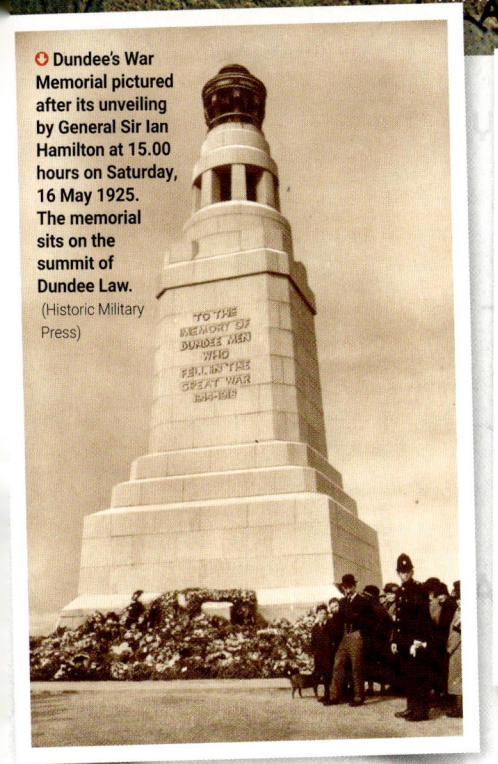

WAR MEMORIALS REMEMBERING THE FALLEN 1914-1918

○ Dundee's War Memorial pictured after its unveiling by General Sir Ian Hamilton at 15.00 hours on Saturday, 16 May 1925. The memorial sits on the summit of Dundee Law. (Historic Military Press)

○ The dedication of Maidstone's War Memorial on 21 June 1922. Located in a square off Tonbridge Road, at the junction with Rocky Hill, the memorial is topped by a bronze statue of St George. (Historic Military Press)

Times were hard for most people in the immediate post-war years and in Wolverhampton, 10 per cent of the money subscribed was allocated to the relief of impecunious widows and other dependents. At West Hartlepool there was a sizeable balance of money remaining after the war memorial had been built which was used to erect sixteen houses and a reading room in the town's Ryehill Gardens.

Worcester's main memorial was entirely utilitarian, in that it consisted of twelve houses erected in Gheluvelt Park for disabled soldiers and sailors. The cenotaph in Rickerby Park, Carlisle, forms one memorial with the park itself, with a new footbridge across the River Eden giving access to the park from the centre of the city.

CHURCH MEMORIALS

For many, especially in smaller communities, the parish church is the only, or at least the most important, public place open to all. Understandably, many war memorials were placed in, on, or around churches. Few things can stir emotions more than music, and a number of churches used the money that had been raised to install new organs.

Such organs were installed at St Gabriel's Church, Cwmbran and Rothley Parish Church in Leicestershire. Usually, a plaque was added to the organs indicating that they were memorials, as was the case in the church at Little Bollington in Cheshire. The plaque there stated the organ had been installed, 'to blend the worship of Almighty God with a grateful memorial of those gallant men of this neighbourhood who fought for the freedom of the world in the Great War 1914-1918'.

A number of memorial organs were dedicated to individuals. A wooden sign on the organ at Chalfont St Giles, Buckinghamshire, reveals that it commemorates a former organist at the church, James E. Mead who was killed, 'whilst succouring the wounded as stretcher-bearer'.

The War Memorial Organ at Crediton Parish Church in Devon has an even closer connection with an organist as it was based on plans drawn in 1915 by the church's own organist, the coincidentally-named Second Lieutenant Harold Organ FRCO, who was sadly killed in action in 1917 aged 28. In 1916 Organ enlisted in the Gloucestershire Regiment; it was with the 4th Battalion that he was killed near Poelcapelle on 9 October 1917. Writing to Second Lieutenant Organ's parents, Major J.D. Newth gave the following account of his death: 'Lieut. Organ was killed leading his men in the same gallant manner that he has always displayed in action since joining the Battalion. While he was giving some orders to his Platoon Sergeant soon after the attack had commenced a bullet ricocheted off his revolver and killed him instantly.' The plans for the organ were completed by Organ's successor, Cyril Church, with it being dedicated on Wednesday, 16 November 1921.

It has to be noted, that not all war memorial organs were installed in parish churches. Many are in non-conformist places of worship, like the one in the Queen Street Methodist Hall in Scarborough which was commissioned by its female members to

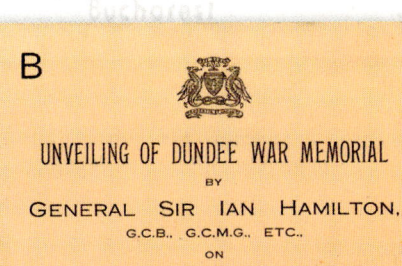

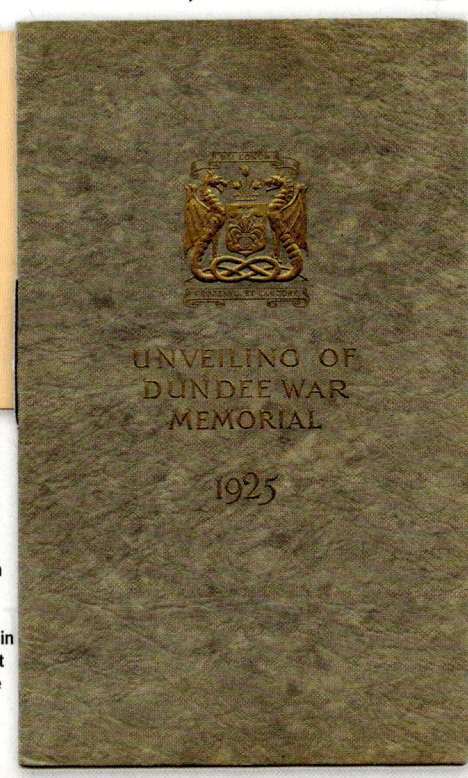

○○ An invitation to, and programme for, the unveiling of Dundee's War Memorial. A hand-written entry on the first page of the programme indicates that it belonged to Mrs Ann Donegan, the next of kin of Corporal 8900 Alexander Donegan MM. Serving in the 7th Battalion Cameron Highlanders, Donegan was shot and killed by a German sniper on 20 August 1917. Aged 24, he is remembered on the Tyne Cot Memorial. The Great War Dundee website states that 'Donegan was a regular soldier who had originally served with the 1st Battalion, arriving in France in August 1914'. An obituary notice in *The Courier* noted that Corporal Donegan 'had seen seven years' service with the regular forces, and proceeded to France on the outbreak of hostilities. He had been twice wounded, and had been awarded the Military Medal.' (Historic Military Press)

REMEMBERING THE FALLEN 45

REMEMBERING THE FALLEN 1914-1918 KNOWN UNTO GOD

Another functional war memorial, much used by adults and pupils alike, is this seat in the main quadrangle at Christ's Hospital School near Horsham in West Sussex. It commemorates former pupils of the school who gave their lives. The two figures represent a young soldier, on the left, and a pupil in the school's traditional uniform. (Historic Military Press)

Located on Nanny Hill in Stocksbridge near Sheffield, the Stocksbridge Memorial Clocktower commemorates 107 men. Unveiled on 1 December 1923 by the Bishop of Sheffield, this image was taken during the Remembrance Day service the following year. (Historic Military Press)

commemorate not only the fallen but also as a thanksgiving for those men who served and returned safely to their womenfolk.

Another, not uncommon form of war memorial erected in churches, was in the form of a new lectern; a notable example of this is that at All Saints in Sudbury, where an angel carved in oak supports the desk. In other instances, the memorial is in the form of panelling on the interior walls of the church or of a screen, either one that already stood in the church or one that purposefully erected.

LET THE BELLS RING OUT

Bells had a particular relevance to the memory of the First World War, as the triumphal announcement of the end of the fighting was marked by the pealing of church bells across the land. Unsurprisingly, therefore, a number of bells were installed, recast or re-hung as a memorial the lost men

A remarkable, and unusual, war memorial – the Coalbrook/Jackfield Memorial Bridge in Shropshire. In the centre of the bridge, which was completed in 1922, a plaque was installed listing the names of those who made the final sacrifice in addition to which, at each end, a plaque was placed. The communities of Coalbrook and Jackfield stood on either side the River Severn. Workers needing to access the further shore had to pay to use a ferry. Not only was this an expense, it could also be hazardous, especially when the river was in flood. The decision was made to use the money raised for a memorial to build a footbridge across the Severn allowing people free access to each side. (Courtesy of John M; www.geograph.org.uk)

KNOWN UNTO GOD REMEMBERING THE FALLEN 1914-1918

of the congregation, with an explanatory plaque placed in the church. There were also instances of the names of the fallen being inscribed upon a commemorative bell. This happened at the Memorial Community Church in Plaistow, London, where the names of 197 men were inscribed on the peal of ten bells which were unveiled in 1925.

A traditional method of celebrating past lives in churches across the UK is that of recording them in stained glass windows. Many parish churches adopted this method of commemoration, often incorporating an image of St George, the warrior saint. More usually seen is the Roll of Honour inscribed on a plaque of wood or stone nearby where the names can more easily be read.

Outside churches, there were instances of memorial lychgates being erected at the entrance to churchyards, with the names of the fallen being inscribed on the low walls supporting the roof of the structure. The

○ The Scottish National War Memorial at Edinburgh Castle being unveiled by HRH the Prince of Wales on 19 July 1927. (Historic Military Press)

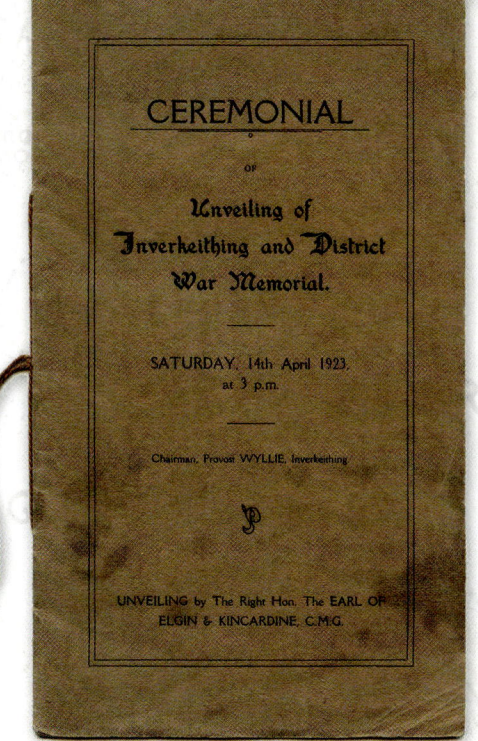

○ The order of service for the unveiling of Inverkeithing War Memorial on Saturday, 14 April 1923. The service was led by the Earl of Elgin and Kincardine. (Historic Military Press)

symbolism in such cases was that many of those that had been killed had passed through those gates, never to return.

Some churches, including St Nicholas at Ringwould in Kent, and Holy Trinity in Northampton, had clocks installed on their towers. But clock-based war memorials were not just confined to places of worship. Clock towers were quite a popular choice in Wales, with five on the island of Anglesey alone. At Senghenydd, near Caerphilly a clock tower was erected as a memorial to the sixty-three men from the community who lost their lives in the First World War and, at Blaenavon, a clock tower stands near the Workmen's Hall, its square-based column has clock faces on all four sides with inscribed plaques on three of them. In Scotland, seven members of the Hearts football team are amongst those remembered on the Memorial Clock that was erected in Edinburgh's Haymarket in 1922.

The more usual village or town structures seen around the country and instantly recognisable as war memorials, are often quite unique, displaying Celtic, Gothic or Eleanor crosses. There are cenotaphs modelled on that in Whitehall, there are obelisks, columns, towers, avenues and circles of trees. There are roads of remembrance, gardens of remembrance, bridges, college cloisters and temples.

The Dorset village of Corfe Castle has a memorial arch with the inscription 'Do'set men don't sheäme their kind' – described by the author and historian Sir J.A. Hammerton as 'one of the few examples of the use of dialect'. In one Highland glen is a rough block of granite marked simply with the figures 1914-1918; it is enough, its message is clear. At Cnoc-a-Clachan,

ORGANISATIONAL MEMORIALS

At Chatham is the memorial of the Royal Engineers, and an obelisk to the Dover Patrol which defended the Channel overlooks St Margret's Bay. The Royal Military College at Sandhurst has a renovated memorial chapel. A Boy Scouts memorial stands at the hilltop village of Loose, near Maidstone, and Tonbridge School has a Gate of Remembrance. At Stratford-on-Avon actors

○ A somewhat unusual memorial, the Ypres Milestone stands just inside the churchyard of Christ Church in Shooter's Hill within the Royal Borough of Greenwich. (Courtesy of Robert Mitchell)

REMEMBERING THE FALLEN 47

REMEMBERING THE FALLEN 1914-1918 WAR MEMORIALS

○ A tissue souvenir programme produced to commemorate the Prince of Wales unveiling the Welsh War Memorial in Cardiff on 12 June 1928. (Historic Military Press)

recorded … [It was] agreed that the unveiling should be carried out by an ex-serviceman and after a Committee ballot Sergeant Eames, who had been blinded at the battle of the Somme, and Private Robert Cruickshank, who had been awarded the Victoria Cross for his actions in Palestine, were chosen. The unveiling took place on 3 December 1921.'

REMEMBERED IN THE LANDSCAPE

In some instances, those who fell, whether individuals or groups, are remembered in the very landscapes they once knew. The wooded cliffs which extend for about a mile along the River Trent from Radcliffe in Northamptonshire, for example, was presented to the village by Mr Lisle Rockley, whose only son, Second Lieutenant William Rockley MC, was killed, aged 21, on 11 October 1918. Serving in the 10th Battalion, York and Lancaster Regiment, William lost his life during the Battle of Passchendaele.

Of Purley's two memorials, one is at Upper Woodcote. As Sir J.A. Hammerton noted, it 'is a road, a third of a mile long, named Promenade de Verdun. For it ten tons of soil came from a sacred spot near Armentières, and from this soil two sacks of shrapnel and pieces of bullets were sifted before it was laid down'.

Near the village of Fovant, to the south of the A30, that once-great south-west road which joins London with the West Country, are a series of magnificent carvings in the chalk of the Wiltshire Downs. During the First World War thousands of men from all parts of the United Kingdom and Commonwealth were stationed for a while in the area before passing on to the Western Front, many never to return.

The first badge created on the Downs was that of the London Rifle Brigade which was cut during 1916. It was formed on the hillside below Chislebury Iron Age hill fort. Regimental records state that a number of young soldiers, having served on the Western Front, arrived as 'walking wounded' at the military hospital at Fovant and, after convalescence, and having entered re-training for further service, they decided to cut an outline of their cap badge on the downs close to their camp. It was the start of

have a memorial of their own in the town's old church.

Other schools and colleges around the country proudly displayed war memorials. At Eton, four tapestries were hung on the walls of the chapel, and Wellington College built a memorial chapel, while Radley College on the Thames erected a memorial archway. The Cheltenham College memorial took the form of cloisters linking the chapel and school buildings, whilst Tonbridge School erected a Gate of Remembrance through which the pupils passed each day in silence.

Companies also introduced their own memorials. The management of staff of the Doulton & Co. factory in Hawkhead Road, Paisley, for example, erected a stunning ceramic memorial in 'honour of the men from these works who fell in the Great War 1914-1918'. When the factory was closed in 1939, the memorial was moved to nearby Hawkhead Cemetery.

The soap manufacturers Lever Brothers, for its part, opted for a memorial on a somewhat grander scale. The design of a bronze sculptural group and relief panels with a granite cross on a plinth with radiating steps was inspired by Lord Leverhulme, the philanthropist owner of Lever Brothers. The memorial was erected in Port Sunlight village. As the Historic England listing for the memorial notes, 'just over 4,000 Lever employees served in the First World War; by its conclusion over 503 had been killed. Initially, Lever had asserted his desire that all those who had served should be listed on the memorial, but this was obviously not possible, so only the names of those who died are

○ The Fovant Badges today. From left to right the badges are those of the Royal Wiltshire Yeomanry, 6th Battalion City of London Regiment, Australian Commonwealth Military Forces, Royal Corps of Signals, the Wiltshire Regiment, the London Rifle Brigade, the Post Office Rifles, and the Devonshire Regiment. (Shutterstock)

48 REMEMBERING THE FALLEN

WAR MEMORIALS **REMEMBERING THE FALLEN 1914-1918**

⊕ The memorial plaque on the summit of Great Gable in the Lake District. (Stewart Smith Photography/Shutterstock)

an honorary member of the Fell and Rock Climbing Club, donated the mountain 'in perpetual memory of the men of the Lake District who fell for God and King, for freedom, peace and right in the Great War'.

Founded in 1906, the Fell and Rock Climbing Club expanded on Baron Leconfield's gesture and purchased a large area of the Lake District above the 1,500 feet contour. This area, which amounted to some 3,000 acres and included no less than twelve fells in the great lakes, was also gifted to the National Trust in October 1923.

A dedication ceremony, described at the time as a 'service in the clouds', was held on top of Great Gable on 8 June 1924. During this, a plaque commemorating twenty members of the Club who lost their lives in the First World War was unveiled. The service was led by author, poet and renowned British mountaineer Geoffrey Winthrop Young. Young had continued to tackle famous peaks after being wounded and losing a leg whilst

a tradition which by the Armistice saw some twenty badges being created over Compton, Fovant and Sutton Downs.

Said to be the largest concentration of chalk carvings in Europe, the Fovant Badges as they are known today consist of twelve surviving carvings in three distinct locations. The main group of nine is that which overlooks Fovant itself. To the east, overlooking Compton Chamberlayne, is the map of Australia, whilst to the west, near Sutton Mandeville, are the badges of the 7th Battalion, City of London Regiment and the Royal Warwickshire Regiment.

It is near the Scottish border in Cumberland that one of the United Kingdom's most impressive memorials can be found – a 3,000-acre area of the Lake District. In was in the aftermath of the Peace Day celebrations in July 1919 that the Lake District landowner Charles Henry Wyndham, the 3rd Baron Leconfield, gifted Scafell Pike to the National Trust. Lord Leconfield,

⊕ The memorial cairn and plaque on the summit of Scafell Pike, the highest mountain in England, which declares that it was donated to the National Trust in 1919 by Lord Leconfield in memory of the men of the Lake District 'who fell for God and King, for freedom, peace and right in the Great War'. (Courtesy of Stuart and Zoe Algar)

⊕ The impressive Lever Brothers memorial in Port Sunlight Village. (John David Photography/Shutterstock)

serving as an ambulance driver at the Battle of San Gabriele in Italy.

Some 500 people had made the climb to be present at the service. A contemporary account of the event includes the following: 'The gloom and gentle wind-sounds added impressiveness to the occasion. There was no effort at pageantry or emotion; the service was a tribute to memory ... The war-stained Union Jack which flew from HMS *Barham* at the Battle of Jutland, and which at the outset enshrouded the bronze tablet, gave the only touch of colour.'

Eventually, more than 100,000 war memorials of every imaginable description were created in the United Kingdom alone. Whether big or small, functional or artistic, each one serves the same purpose – to ensure that the memory of those who served or fell in the Great War is remembered. ⊕

REMEMBERING THE FALLEN **49**

REMEMBERING THE FALLEN 1914-1918 KNOWN UNTO GOD

KNOWN UNTO GOD

On 11 November 1920, the body of an unidentified British soldier was buried in Westminster Abbey in the presence of King George V.

The gun carriage of the Royal Horse Artillery, drawn by six magnificently-groomed horses, passed slowly through the vast, silent crowds. There was not a sound except for people gently sobbing and the clop of horses' hooves. From Victoria Station and past Hyde Park, the cortege moved along The Mall to Whitehall, stopping at the Cenotaph, which was concealed by two huge Union Flags. King George laid a wreath on the gun carriage and then pressed a button on the top of the pillar in front of him, and the two flags fell to reveal the Cenotaph, the symbolic empty tomb of the missing.

With the King, the Royal Family and ministers of state following, the cortege moved on to Westminster Abbey, where a thousand bereaved women were sitting waiting, their mourning signified by the flowers and wreaths laid on their knees. The casket was unloaded to the soft pealing of a single bell and was borne through the north transept into the West Nave of the Abbey flanked by a guard of honour of 100 recipients of the Victoria Cross. Within the casket were the remains of an unidentified soldier, 'unknown by name or rank', and he was to be buried among kings, statesmen, scientists and poets.

UNKNOWN COMRADE

It was in 1916 that the Reverend David Railton, the curate of Folkestone who had become a temporary chaplain to the Forces, was moved by the sight of a grave near Armentières which was marked with a rough wooden cross inscribed 'An unknown British soldier, of the Black Watch'. For some reason that image, above all the slaughter, suffering and bloodshed – he himself was awarded the Military Cross for saving an officer and two men under heavy fire – remained with him throughout the war.

'How that grave caused me to think!' he later recalled. 'But, who was he, and who were they [his folk]? ... Was he just a laddie ... There was no answer to those questions, nor has there ever been yet. So I thought and thought and wrestled in thought. What can I do to ease the pain of father, mother, brother, sister, sweetheart, wife and friend? Quietly and gradually there came out of the mist of thought this answer clear and strong, "Let this body – this symbol of him – be carried reverently over the sea to his native land". And I was happy for about five or ten minutes.'[1]

After the war Railton was determined to follow through with his idea of what he called an Unknown Comrade being taken from France back to the UK and reburied in a grand public fashion to symbolise the hundreds of thousands of missing men of the British forces. As it happened, something along such lines was already being considered in France.

○ The coffin containing the body of the Unknown Warrior is pictured leaving St Pol-sur-Ternoise near Arras to begin its journey to London. (Historic Military Press)

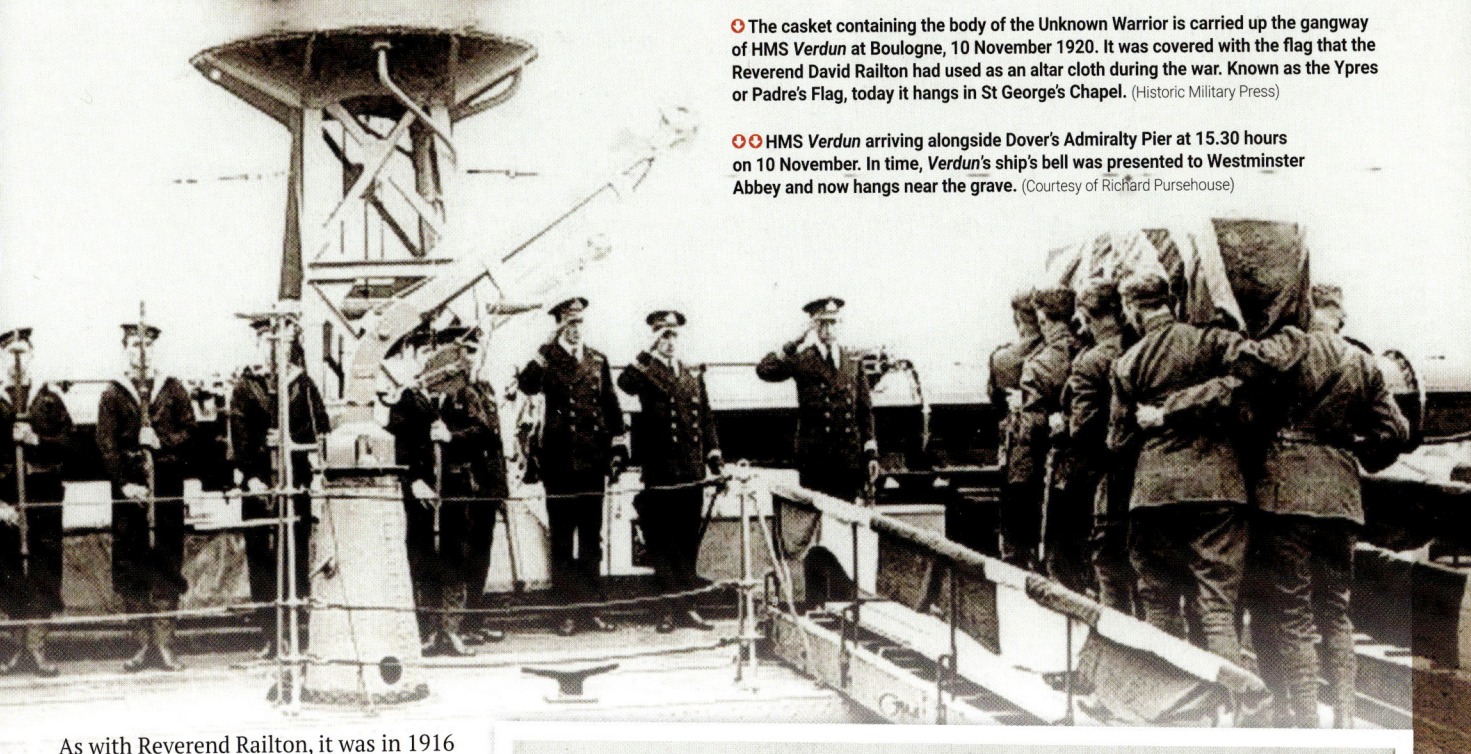

KNOWN UNTO GOD REMEMBERING THE FALLEN 1914-1918

○ **The casket containing the body of the Unknown Warrior is carried up the gangway of HMS *Verdun* at Boulogne, 10 November 1920. It was covered with the flag that the Reverend David Railton had used as an altar cloth during the war. Known as the Ypres or Padre's Flag, today it hangs in St George's Chapel.** (Historic Military Press)

○○ **HMS *Verdun* arriving alongside Dover's Admiralty Pier at 15.30 hours on 10 November. In time, *Verdun*'s ship's bell was presented to Westminster Abbey and now hangs near the grave.** (Courtesy of Richard Pursehouse)

As with Reverend Railton, it was in 1916 that an officer of *Le Souvenir Français* – the French association for maintaining war graves, memorials, 'and memory', and which was comparable to the then Imperial War Graves Commission – proposed the idea of burying 'an ignored soldier' in the Panthéon in Paris where many of the great and the good of France were interred. This proposal was taken up by politicians and a formal bill was presented to the Parlement français in November 1918. The decision was voted into law on September 1919, but rather than in the Panthéon, France's Unknown Soldier would be placed in a tomb under the Arc de Triumph.

With such a precedent in mind, in October 1920 Railton wrote to Herbert Edward Ryle, the Dean of Westminster, with his proposal

○ **A silent guard of Bluejackets watches over the coffin of the Unknown Warrior, with the four wreaths, during the journey to Dover.** (Courtesy of Richard Pursehouse)

to bury an Unknown Comrade in the Abbey. The Dean gave it his full support. In fact, the idea had already been aired in the press, with the *Daily Express* launching a campaign to bury an unknown British soldier beneath the Cenotaph which was under construction in Whitehall. The paper declared that, 'the dust of one soldier, unknown and undistinguished, would lend it a sacredness worthy of so great a monument'.

The scheme was taken up by Lloyd George who persuaded both the King and his Cabinet to back the proposal. On the evening of 15 October, the Lloyd George's secretary replied to Dean Railton: 'Your memorandum ... was considered this afternoon by the Cabinet and accepted in principle. The Prime Minister has already notified the King of this ... I should add that the Cabinet would prefer that the first announcement of the adoption of this

REMEMBERING THE FALLEN **51**

REMEMBERING THE FALLEN 1914-1918 KNOWN UNTO

○ Pall bearers prepare to bring the body of the Unknown Warrior ashore at Dover. (Courtesy of Richard Pursehouse)

○ The coffin is carried down the quayside at Dover to the train waiting in Dover Maritime Station. (Historic Military Press)

proposal should be made in Parliament. The Prime Minister asks me to thank you for this impressive suggestion.'

The Cabinet agreed to set up a committee to arrange the process. The Committee was composed of Lord Curzon, Lord Lee of Fareham, Mr Winston Churchill, Mr Walter Long and Sir Alfred Mond, with Colonel Storr of the Foreign Office to act as the Secretary.

The French intended to honour their *soldat inconnu* on Armistice Day of that year, and it was hoped that Britain would be able to do the same. There was already a plan in place to unveil the new Cenotaph in Whitehall and to coincide the two events would present a moving and memorable scene. If the Unknown Soldier was to be buried in Westminster Abbey that same day, the Cabinet Committee had just three weeks to have everything arranged and in place.

The Committee turned to the three branches of the armed forces for advice on how to proceed, and it was agreed that it was just possible in the time available to organise the exhumation of an unknown body and put all the arrangements in place to have the body taken back to the UK. The decision was made to call the unidentified man the Unknown Warrior. With the upheaval of the Russian Revolution all too fresh in people's minds, the term 'comrade' was seen as being too politically sensitive to be used. The term 'warrior' was seen as being sufficiently neutral, and could apply equally to a soldier, sailor or airman.

The Committee eventually declared that: 'The remains of one of the numerous unknown men who fell and were buried in France, should be exhumed; conveyed to England; if necessary, cremated; escorted by soldiers as a military funeral procession to Westminster Abbey, and there, after a short, impressive funeral service, be buried in the Nave, a central position having been granted by the Dean, fairly opposite the great West Door, so as to be easily seen and identified by people in all future times.'

The inscription on the coffin was to read: 'A British Warrior Who Fell in the Great War 1914-18 For King and Country'.

○ Once in the station at Dover, the coffin was placed in railway wagon No.132, which had been decorated with laurels, palms and lilies, and four sentries, one from each Service, stood guard until the time for departure. A prototype luggage van that entered service in 1919, No.132 was the South Eastern & Chatham Railway's most modern van – and it was for this reason that it was chosen. In fact, on previous occasions this wagon had been used to carry the bodies of Nurse Edith Cavell (which is why it is today known as 'The Cavell Van') and Captain Fryatt. Wagon No.132 has survived and can be seen today on the Kent and East Sussex Railway. (Courtesy of Michael Roots)

○ The interior of Wagon No.132 decorated to appear as it would have looked during its journey to London on 10 November 1920. A passenger coach was also attached to the train for use by the escort of one officer and fifteen men. It was at 17.50 hours that the special train pulled out of Dover Marine Station. The *Daily Mail* reported: 'The train thundered through the dark, wet, moonless night. At the platforms by which it rushed could be seen groups of women watching and silent, many dressed in deep mourning. Many an upper window was open, and against the golden square of light was silhouetted clear cut and black the head and shoulders of some faithful watcher ... In the London suburbs there were scores of homes with back doors flung wide, light flooding out, and in the garden figures of men, women and children gazing at the great lighted train rushing past.' (Courtesy of Michael Roots)

52 REMEMBERING THE FALLEN

The train which included wagon No.132 arrived at Platform 8 in Victoria Station at 20.32 hours on 10 November. It remained in situ, and under escort, until the following morning. (Historic Military Press)

The gun carriage bearing the Unknown Warrior passing the Cenotaph in Whitehall, 11 November 1920. The procession departed from Victoria at 09.40 hours and travelled via Hyde Park Corner and the Mall to reach the Cenotaph. (Historic Military Press)

IN THE MIDNIGHT HOUR

The man given the job of recovering an unidentified body from among the many British and Imperial dead was Brigadier General L.J. Wyatt, General Officer Commanding British troops in France, and director of the Imperial War Graves Commission.

Considerable lengths were taken to ensure that the identity and origin of the chosen soldier could never be known. On 7 November 1920, four field ambulances, each with an officer and two other ranks drove to cemeteries at each of the main British battle zones of the Western Front – the Aisne, the Somme, Arras and Ypres. Equipped with picks and shovels, each party was instructed to select a grave marked 'Unknown British Soldier' from the early stage of the war, ideally 1914, and exhume the body. They were not told why.

After making their choice and removing the body, the grave was filled in and the exhumed remains were placed in a sack, loaded onto the ambulance and taken to Wyatt's headquarters at St Pol-sur-Ternoise, some twenty miles from Arras. Each ambulance party was given a separate route to St Pol-sur-Ternoise and different arrival schedules so that there was no possibility of them meeting or conferring with each other. After unloading their respective bodies, each party was sent straight back to its unit, still oblivious of the true nature of their unusual task.

The reason why such measures were undertaken was to ensure that no one would ever be able to identify the body of the man who would be selected as the Unknown Warrior. This was to allow every grieving family of missing soldiers to hope that it might be their loved one that was the Unknown Warrior who would be placed alongside the most distinguished and celebrated names in British history. 'The Unknown Warrior whose body was to be buried [in Westminster Abbey] may have been born to high position or to low,' wrote a contemporary, 'he may have been a sailor, a soldier or an airman; an Englishman, a Scotsman, a Welshman, an Irishman, a man of the Dominions, a Sikh, a Gurkha. No-one knows. But he was one who gave his life for the people of the British Empire.'[2]

The four bodies were received at Wyatt's HQ by the Reverend George Kendall OBE, and carefully checked to ensure that there was nothing on any of the bodies that could in any way identify them. The bodies were then each covered by a Union Flag so that outwardly all four appeared exactly the same, and they were laid in a row in the chapel of St Pol. When he had finished his inspection, Reverend Kendall left the chapel and an armed guard was mounted at the door.

At midnight, Brigadier Wyatt, accompanied by Lieutenant Colonel E.A.S. Gell, went into in the small corrugated

Placed on a carriage provided by 'N' Battery RHA, the coffin of the Unknown Warrior is pictured about to leave Victoria Station to travel through the crowd-lined streets of London to Westminster Abbey. The pall bearers who accompanied the coffin were Admiral Lord Beatty, Admiral Sir Hedworth Meux, Admiral Sir Henry Jackson, Admiral Sir C.E. Madden, Field Marshal Lord French, Field Marshal Lord Haig, Field Marshal Lord Methuen, Field Marshal Sir Henry Wilson, General Lord Horne, General Lord Byng, General Albert Farrar-Gatliff and Air Chief Marshal Sir Hugh Trenchard. (Courtesy of Richard Pursehouse)

REMEMBERING THE FALLEN 53

REMEMBERING THE FALLEN 1914-1918 KNOWN UNTO GOD

A drawing depicting King George V during the burial service in Westminster Abbey, 11 November 1920.
(Courtesy of Richard Pursehouse)

spot – allegedly a shell hole on the road to Albert – and reinterred the bodies while the reverend said a simple prayer.

The next morning, 8 November, a service was held in the St Pol chapel with representatives of the Church of England, the Roman Catholic Church and the non-conformist churches present. At midday the body was taken by escort in a well-worn and battered ambulance to Boulogne for the journey to England.

The reason why the four exhumation parties had been told to find bodies from 1914 was to ensure that the remains had decomposed to the degree that only bones were left. The church authorities did not want the smell of putrefying flesh in Westminster Abbey and, despite the Committee stating that cremation could take place if necessary, it was thought that cremating the body before burial would mean that only dust was being interred which would have less poignancy than the bones of an unknown soldier. This was also supported by the Army, as any soldier who was killed in 1914 would be a regular professional, and not one of the civilian volunteers of the Kitchener armies.

All then was set for Armistice Day.

THE FUNERAL FLOTILLA

Throughout the early hours of 10 November, the coffin lay at rest in the library of Boulogne castle, which had been suitably adorned with flowers and wreaths. A guard was mounted outside the library by the French 8ᵉ Régiment d'*Infanterie*.

That same night, a Lieutenant Swift returned from France with barrels containing 100 bags of French soil to be placed in the tomb in Westminster, so that the Unknown Warrior 'might lie in the earth so many gave their lives for'.

At 10.00 hours, the British undertakers who had taken the coffin to France placed it in a casket of English oak made from trees that grew in the grounds of Hampton Court Palace. The casket was sealed with two wrought-iron straps. A 16th century crusader's sword, a gift from the King and which came from the Tower of London collection, was also attached to the seal.

The casket was then taken down to the port, with the mile-long cortege passing through the packed streets of the town to the strains of a military band playing Chopin's *Funeral March*. Children had been given the day off school and they joined the townspeople lining the streets which were adorned with flags and streamers and flanked by French soldiers with arms reversed.

On the dockside, Marshal Foch gave a speech praising the fortitude and bravery of British soldiers. The coffin was duly carried aboard HMS *Verdun*, along with four wreaths so large that it took four soldiers to lift each of them. Foch walked almost to the water's edge alone and saluted the Unknown Warrior as the warship moved off from the quayside at a little after midday.

To the sound of a resounding salute from a Royal Navy guard and the guns of the French shore batteries, *Verdun* rendezvoused with a flotilla of escorting destroyers out at sea. The latter, six in total, took up positions three in line ahead and three in line astern. All of the warships had their flags at half-mast.

Setting off across the Channel, the funeral flotilla was off Dover by 13.00 hours on what was a typically grey November day. *Verdun* remained off Dover until 15.00 hours, at which time she sailed alone into the harbour through the eastern entrance. A nineteen-gun salute from the ramparts of the castle

iron hut which served as the chapel. Wyatt then placed his hand on one of the identical bodies. 'I had no idea even of the area from which the body I selected had come, and no-one else can know it.' The two men then placed the body Wyatt had selected into a plain coffin of English pine which stood in front of the altar, and the lid was screwed down.

The three remaining bodies were at once taken away and reinterred in the St Pol British Cemetery – at least that it the official version. Another account states that the bodies were taken to a part of the old front line where there had been much heavy fighting and which was still littered with shell craters and the remains of old trenches. The burial party chose a suitable

Members of the public pay their respects at the grave of the Unknown Warrior following the burial service.
(Historic Military Press)

Propped up on a stand, the coffin is seen here in Westminster Abbey. The inner coffin shell was made by Walter Jackson of the firm of Ingall, Parsons & Clive Forward at Harrow, North London, and the larger coffin was supplied by the undertakers in charge of the arrangements, Nodes & Son. The ironwork and coffin plate were made by D.J. Williams of the Brunswick Ironworks at Caernarfon in Wales. (Historic Military Press)

54 REMEMBERING THE FALLEN

signalled the arrival of the destroyer carrying the Unknown Warrior. Shops had been closed for the day and people watched the from the cliffs to the east and west and at every point around the harbour where they could glimpse a little of the unfolding drama.

HMS *Verdun* berthed at the Admiralty Pier, where so many of the wounded from the battlefields had been disembarked. Six warrant officers from the Royal Navy, Royal Marines, the Army and the RAF went onboard the destroyer and carried the coffin ashore to the mournful wail of bo'suns' pipes. A procession, led by Lieutenant General Sir George MacDonogh, Adjutant-General to the Forces, formed ahead and behind the coffin as it was transferred the 100 yards to the Dover Marine railway station.

The coffin was placed inside a carriage of the South-Eastern and Chatham Railway which was lined with purple cloth and decorated with flowers. Inside were placed the four huge wreaths. The carriage had been painted white so that it could be easily spotted as it made its way through the countryside of southern England during the journey to Victoria Station in London where it rested overnight.

ARMISTICE DAY

On the morning of 11 November, the coffin was placed on a gun carriage drawn by six black horses and began its journey through the crowd-lined streets, making its first stop by the Cenotaph. Then the carriage and pall bearers, followed by the King, members of the Royal Family and ministers of State, made its way to the north door of Westminster Abbey.

From the altar inside Westminster Abbey came the faint murmur of the precentor intoning the Lord's Prayers. The moment had come. 'Silence. The bell [Big Ben] tolled eleven, one heavy stroke after another, and at once all of us in the church became part of the multitude outside, united in the same mood,' wrote one of those there at that momentous occasion, Francis Perrot. 'Out there in the street some loud word of command followed the last stroke. All sound ceased in a strange intensity of stillness. For two minutes it lasted … The cathedral seemed to breathe as in sleep.'[3]

Eight Grenadier Guardsmen bore the coffin into the Abbey, to be taken by pall-bearers – soldiers on one side, sailors on the other – towards its resting place, which had been carefully measured so as to disturb only as much of the sacred ground as was necessary, as nineteen guns in Hyde Park fired the Field Marshal's salute. Down the parallel lines of blue and khaki the Unknown Warrior was carried.

After the coffin had been lowered into the grave, the barrels of Flanders earth were poured over it. A large slab of black Tournai marble was then placed on top. As the Unknown Warrior was finally laid to rest, there was a roll of drums, then the clear bugle call of reveille to signify that life goes on. The service was over.

As he left the Abbey, the King looked down at the Unknown Warrior, as did the other dignitaries who followed him. This broke the spell of silence, and the congregation left their seats to crowd round the grave, the Victoria Cross recipients paying their respects to a fallen comrade. 'Then the women left their seats and began that long file past of the bereaved that was to last through the day,' continued Francis Perrot. 'A woman plucked a white chrysanthemum from a bunch she carried and threw it into the tomb. This example was quickly followed, and soon the purple carpet was thickly scattered with flowers white and red.'

◉ Two views of the grave of the Unknown Warrior at the west end of the Nave of Westminster Abbey. It is covered by a slab of black Belgian marble from a quarry near Namur, the inscription on which was composed by Herbert Ryle when he was Dean of Westminster. (Historic Military Press)

◉ General Pershing, on behalf of the United States of America, conferred the Congressional Medal of Honor on the Unknown Warrior on 17 October 1921. Accompanied by the Duke of Connaught, General Pershing is seen here inspecting the Guard of Honour before entering Westminster Abbey on that occasion. The medal now hangs in a frame on a pillar near the grave. (Library of Congress; LC-USZ62-66427)

NOTES
1. *The Unknown Warrior* 'Unknown and yet well known' Compiled by Mary P. Wilkinson, (Imperial War Museum, London, 2000).
2. Quoted, unsourced, in Neil Hanson, *The Unknown Soldier, The Story of the Missing of the Great War* (Doubleday, London, 2005), p.355.
3. Francis Perrot, 'The King was Chief Mourner At the Burial of the Unknown Warrior', *The Great War... I Was There! Undying Memories of 1914-1918* (Hammerton, London), p.1933.

REMEMBERING THE FALLEN 1914-1918 A SYMBOL OF REMEMBRANCE

A SYMBOL OF REMEMBRANCE

In the spring of 1915, a Canadian officer, John McCrae, was inspired by the sight of poppies growing in battle-scarred fields to write the now famous poem *In Flanders Fields*. McCrae's words helped ensure that the poppy was adopted as an international symbol of Remembrance.

This remarkable art installation, named *Blood Swept Lands and Seas of Red* after the first line of a poem by an unknown First World War soldier, was created in the moat of the Tower of London in 2014 to commemorate the centenary of the start of the war. It consisted of 888,246 ceramic red poppies, each intended to represent one British or Colonial serviceman killed in the conflict. (AC Manley/Shutterstock)

A portrait of John McCrae circa 1914. (Courtesy of Guelph Museums, McCrae House)

SYMBOL OF REMEMBRANCE **REMEMBERING THE FALLEN 1914-1918**

Just a few dozen yards away lay the enemy front line. In between was nought but craters and mud and maybe, just maybe, a shattered tree stump or two. Yet, amidst this tortured, twisted landscape of grey and brown, of death and despair, was a tiny flutter of brilliant colour. Where nothing could survive, the blood-red petals of the corn poppy waved poignantly in the breeze. A sign then of new life, a symbol now of remembrance.

It may seem odd that the poppy should flourish where nothing else could live. The reason for this is that the poppy seeds, laying dormant in the soil, were exposed to the light they needed for germination when the earth was thrown up by the exploding shells and mines. The poppy, normally considered a weed, grows readily in corn fields where the soil is turned annually. Though the corn, along with almost everything else, was

REMEMBERING THE FALLEN

destroyed by the shelling and explosions, the hardy poppy seeds survived – to blossom profusely in the craters and along the banks of the trenches of the Western Front during the First World War.

This, of course, was not a new phenomenon. In Europe's previous great conflict, the Napoleonic Wars, the cannonballs and shells of that era also churned up the battlefields allowing the poppies to make their dramatic appearance. Likewise, poppies grow in many countries around the world and the Flanders poppy can also be found in Turkey where, in April 1915 when the Allied forces landed at Gallipoli, the brilliant red flowers filled the often-barren landscape. When men fought and died, wherever in the world, the poppy marked their passing.

It was in that same year, 1915, that the humble poppy was immortalised in a simple verse published in the magazine *Punch*. Entitled *In Flanders Fields*, it has become one of the most memorable poems of the First World War.

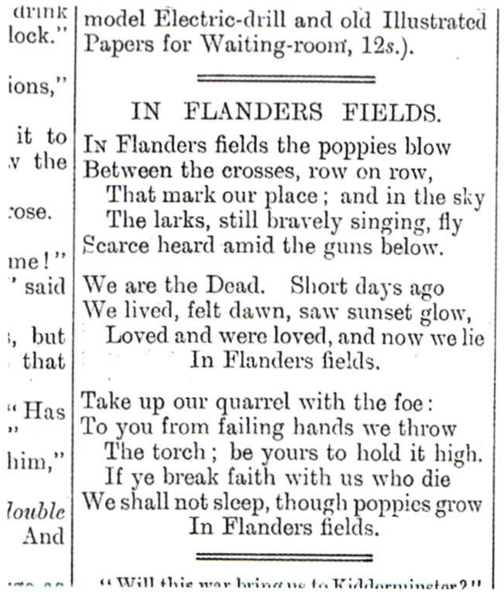

○ The kind of disturbed ground on the battlefields of the First World War in which poppies thrived. This picture shows personnel from No.1 Printing Company, Royal Engineers, some still asleep, in a support trench near Beaumont Hamel on the first day of the Battle of the Somme, 1 July 1916. (Historic Military Press)

○ A cutting showing how *In Flanders Fields* first appeared in *Punch* during December 1915. (Historic Military Press)

The poet who penned these words was a Canadian poet, physician, author, artist and soldier, John McCrae. Having been appointed as the Medical Officer and Major of the 1st Brigade Canadian Field Artillery, at 03.30 hours on 23 April 1915, McCrae accompanied the brigade as it moved up to positions along the Yser Canal, on the front line two miles north of Ypres. It was the beginning of 'seventeen days of Hades'.

Days and nights with no sleep followed, with a constant stream of casualties interspersed with serving the guns. Although he recorded gruesome details in his diaries, a letter to his mother told simply of how he had sheltered terrified dogs, of birdsong heard over the tumult of trench warfare, and of the scent of spring flowers, with no mention of gas.

McCrae's Commanding Officer, Edward Morrison, a newspaper editor in peacetime, set the scene: 'HQ was in a trench on the top of the bank of the Ypres Canal. John had his dressing station in a hole dug in the foot of the bank. During periods in the battle men who were shot actually rolled down the bank into his dressing station. Along from us a few hundred yards was the headquarters of a regiment, and many times during the battle John and I watched them burying their dead whenever there was a lull. Thus the crosses, row on row, grew into a good-sized cemetery.'

McCrae himself wrote that for, 'For seventeen days and seventeen nights none of us have had our clothes off, nor our boots even, except occasionally. In all that time while I was awake, gunfire and rifle fire never ceased for sixty seconds.... And behind it all was the constant background of the sights of the dead, the wounded, the maimed, and a terrible anxiety lest the line should give way.'

○ This First World War bunker is located beside Essex Farm Cemetery north of Ypres. It was in this spot that an Advanced Dressing Station existed at the time of McCrae's presence, and, though his grave is lost, it is believed that Lieutenant Helmer was buried in Essex Farm Cemetery. Because of its links with John McCrae, the area known as Essex Farm is now one of the most visited locations within the Ypres Salient. (Historic Military Press)

A SYMBOL OF REMEMBRANCE REMEMBERING THE FALLEN 1914-1918

Early in the morning of Sunday, 2 May 1915, Lieutenant Owen Hague and Lieutenant Alexis Helmer, the latter a close friend of McCrae, were on their way to check on a Canadian artillery battery located on the bank of the Yser Canal near St. Julien. They had only gone a few yards when a six-inch, high explosive artillery shell burst near them.[1]

Helmer, a popular young 22-year-old officer in the Canadian Field Artillery, was killed instantly. His remains were gathered up in sandbags and safety-pinned in a blanket for the funeral, which was conducted in the dark. McCrae noted the funeral in his diary, and, with no prayer book, conducted the service from memory. Hague, a 26-year-old serving with 7th Battery 2nd Brigade Canadian Field Artillery, survived a little longer, only to succumb to his wounds later the same day at a Field Hospital near Hazebrouck.

It was after Helmer's funeral that while delivering the brigade's mail Colour Sergeant Major Cyril Allinson observed

○ Depicting a lone soldier standing in a field of poppies looking at a grave, this savings poster used a line from McCrae's *In Flanders Fields* to encourage people to purchase Victory Bonds.

○ A portrait of Private John Oldham. Hailing from Streatham in London, Oldham had worked as a plumber's mate and in the civil service prior to enlisting on 6 September 1914. Having served on the Somme, he was gassed – so badly that 'when the doctor tapped him on the chest he fainted' – and, suffering from Shell Shock, was discharged from the Army as unfit in May 1917. (Courtesy of John Oldhan; www.europeana14-18)

○ A pressed poppy in a First World War veteran's bible. The pair belonged to Private John Oldham, 23rd (County of London) Battalion, London Regiment, who brought both items back from France. (Courtesy of John Oldhan; www.europeana14-18)

○ A sketch of poppies from John McCrae's sketchbook. (Courtesy of Guelph Museums, McCrae House)

McCrae writing a poem in pencil on a message pad whilst sitting on the rear steps of an ambulance, still more or less under fire. The first draft, entitled *We Shall Not Sleep*, took about ten minutes. Allinson himself then wrote: 'The poem was an exact description of the scene in front of us both. He used the word blow in that line because the poppies actually were being blown that morning by a gentle east wind. It never occurred to me at that time that it would ever be published. It seemed to me just an exact description of the scene. He looked around, his eyes straying to the grave.'

McCrae was seemingly unsatisfied and discarded his work. Morrison, however, recovered it, and went on to note: 'This poem was born of fire and blood during the hottest phase of the second battle of Ypres.'

Through circumstances that have never been fully explained, as accounts vary, McCrae was pursued to submit the poem for publication. *In Flanders Fields* duly appeared anonymously in the edition of *Punch* that was published on 8 December 1915, though in the index to that year McCrae was duly acknowledged as the author. The verses swiftly became one of the most popular poems of the war, being republished throughout the world. It rapidly becoming synonymous with the sacrifice of the soldiers who died in the conflict and in the years since the Armistice has become a symbol of Remembrance in its own right.

In 1918, the poem inspired Moina Michael, a professor at the University of Georgia in the United States, to always wear a poppy as a symbol of remembrance, and to write a similar poem of her own, entitled, *We Shall Keep the Faith*. Miss Michael had taken leave of absence from the university to volunteer to assist in the New York-based training headquarters for overseas YWCA workers. As the war was coming to an end Moina Michael, determined to promote the Flanders poppy as a physical symbol of remembrance, supplied, at her own expense the flowers for the hall in which the Twenty-fifth Conference of the Overseas YMCA War Secretaries was taking place on 9 November 1918 – and, of course, the flowers she chose were poppies.

It was one thing to think of poppies, but quite another to find them in the heart of New York, so she looked for artificial ones. 'That Saturday afternoon,' she wrote, 'I went down poppy hunting in New York City. ➜

REMEMBERING THE FALLEN **59**

REMEMBERING THE FALLEN 1914-1918 A SYMBOL OF REMEMBRANCE

After the Conference, the attendees went up to Miss Michael to ask if they could also wear one of her poppies. Each one, proudly sporting a red poppy, then returned to their duties in France. By the first week of December the Overseas YMCA Workers had elected to adopt the poppy as its emblem, informing Miss Michael that, 'in recognition of the brave men of Flanders who gave their lives in devotion to a great cause on the Fields of Flanders where the Poppies grow. It will be a constant reminder to us that we too must give our lives unsparingly in service.'

FLANDERS MEMORIAL POPPY SYMBOL

After the war, Miss Michael returned to her post at the University. On her return to Georgia she found that after the initial celebrations at the return of the first American troops to the US, the men, and the sacrifices they had made, were largely forgotten and often the jobs which they had been promised would still be theirs after the war had been given to others, while some were too incapacitated to work. 'Our men had gone several thousand miles to conquer the infernal regions turned loose from the North Sea to the Mediterranean,' she wrote. 'They crossed waters whose lurking submarines might send them to an unmarked grave beneath the waves. The supreme service had been demanded of them – and now such an indifference finally settled around and over all as to their mental, physical and spiritual needs.'

This reinvigorated her mission to have some national emblem of remembrance. During February and March 1919, she sent out thousands of letters to the leaders of every religious, patriotic and educational group listed in the United States, explaining the purpose of what had become called the Flanders Memorial Poppy Symbol. As the concept of the poppy as a symbol of remembrance appeared to be generating considerable appeal, Moina Michael sought to gain some official status for her idea. As an idea could not be patented, she made use of a long-standing friendship by writing to her Georgia Congressman, Charles H. Brand, asking if he could persuade the War Department to promote the poppy as an emblem 'to be worn by all the nations as a tribute to those who have fought for and won the victory'.

At the same time, she tried to gain support for her idea through the commercial world,

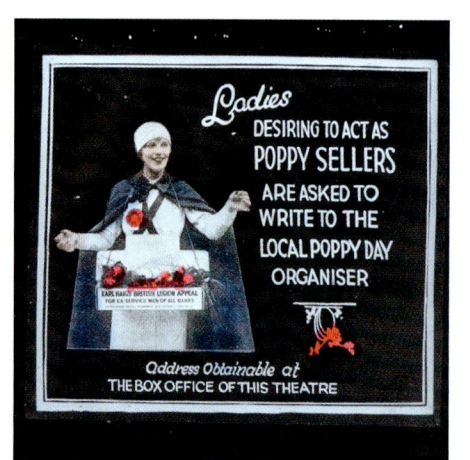

○ A Haig Fund Poppy seller. The image was taken in Crewkerne, Somerset. (Historic Military Press)

After visiting several novelty shops which featured artificial flowers and failing to find red poppies, I went to Wanamaker's. After searching in the flower collections, I found a large red poppy, which I bought for my desk bud-vase and two dozen small silk red four-petaled poppies, fashioned after the wild poppies of Flanders. Having made the purchase, I told the pretty little Jewess, who served me, why I was searching for single petaled red poppies. She was quite sympathetic, for her brother was then sleeping among the poppies behind the battle lines of France in a few-months' old soldier's grave. This personal contact with such a personal reaction further convinced me that this choice of a remembrance emblem for those sleeping in Flanders Fields was no accident but a logical one.'²

○ Taken during the 1920s, this image depicts three brothers, possibly veterans, wearing Remembrance poppies. (Historic Military Press)

○ A young poppy seller in the United States. The original caption, dated 24 May 1929, states: 'Gloria Guguere of 3406 W. 136th Street probably the youngest of all poppy sellers, stopped Patrolman Andrew Bessick yesterday and persuaded him to take time off duty to purchase a veterans of foreign wars poppy.' (Historic Military Press)

○ Two original glass plate adverts appealing for poppy sellers. Produced in the years after the First World War, these would have been used in places such as cinemas. (Historic Military Press)

60 REMEMBERING THE FALLEN

A SYMBOL OF REMEMBRANCE REMEMBERING THE FALLEN 1914-1918

which led to a meeting with a designer in New York, Mr Lee Keedick, who agreed to design a national emblem. Before the end of 1918 he had produced a final design, which Miss Michael accepted. This emblem consisted of a border of blue on a white background with the Torch of Liberty and a Poppy entwined in the centre, containing the colours of the Allied flags: red, white, blue, black, green and yellow.

The 'Torch and Poppy' emblem was first used officially on 14 February 1919, in Carnegie Hall, New York City. The event was a lecture given by the Canadian pilot, Colonel William Avery 'Billy' Bishop VC, CB, DSO & Bar, MC DFC, ED. His lecture was titled *Air Fighting in Flanders Fields*. As the lecture ended a large flag with the new torch and poppy emblem on it was unfurled at the back of the stage.[3]

The press also printed stories about the poppy symbol, one of the most impressive, at least visually, was published in the Sunday edition of the *Sandusky Register* of 6 April 1919. This article included a double-column photograph of Miss Michael and the poppy garden which had been planted in Sandusky, Ohio, in the form of the Flanders poppy symbol. The New York *Tribune* also carried a feature detailing the Flanders Victory Memorial Flag which had been adopted by the Calvary Baptist Church, which included the Torch of Liberty entwined with poppies.

However, the poppy emblem was not taken up by the US War Department and despite Miss Michael's continued efforts to promote her idea, no other official government body supported her scheme. Due to the lack of interest, Lee Keedick dropped out of the joint venture. The remembrance poppy, it seemed, was wilting.

○ A Haig Fund poppy seller pictured in the Field of Remembrance, Westminster, 11 November 1938. The original caption states: 'The Field of Remembrance close to the North Door of Westminster Abbey has in recent years become almost as important on Armistice Day as the Cenotaph. [Here] ex-Private H.E. Day, of the 15th Hussars, who lost a leg in the war, is standing in the Field of Remembrance in the early dawn of November 11, 1938, selling the little wooden crosses with a poppy attached which are planted in the grass plot by relations and friends of the dead.' (Historic Military Press)

○ Silk poppies being manufactured at the factory in n Petersham Road, Richmond, during the 1930s. (Historic Military Press)

JOBS FOR THE GIRLS – AND THE BOYS

In the summer of 1919, Miss Michael taught a class of disabled ex-servicemen and witnessing their need (many hundreds of veterans applied for the classes), decided to abandon academia to focus all her efforts at promoting the Flanders Memorial Poppy in the hope that it would bring recognition to the returned soldiers who could not undertake normal work.

On 19 August 1920, she approached the convention of Georgia Department of the American Legion and presented her Memorial Poppy material. This time her efforts flowered, and the poppy symbol was taken up as the emblem of the National American Legion. There was a representative of the French YMCA Secretariat at the convention, Madame Anna E. Guérin, and she suggested that the women of France could make artificial poppies to sell in the United States to raise money for the rehabilitation of the devastated regions of France.

REMEMBERING THE FALLEN **61**

REMEMBERING THE FALLEN 1914-1918 A SYMBOL OF REMEMBRANCE

POPPY MANUFACTURING

A poppy being manufactured for a recent Remembrance Day. The Royal British Legion continues to provide financial, social and emotional support to millions who have served and are currently serving in the Armed Forces, and their dependents. Nearly 10.5 million people are currently eligible for its support and they receive thousands of calls for help every year. To find out more about the Legion's work, or support the Poppy Appeal, visit: www.britishlegion.org.uk
(Courtesy of the Royal British Legion)

◯ A similar project to that pictured at the start of this article, the artwork seen here, called *Wave*, was unveiled at the CWGC's Plymouth Naval Memorial on Wednesday, 23 August 2017. (Apogee Images/Shutterstock)

◯ The front and rear of a five-petal fabric poppy with card stem. This is believed to be a wartime economy version issued from 1942 until 1944. (Historic Military Press)

Madame Guérin founded the American and French Children's League through which she quickly organized French women, children and war veterans to make artificial poppies out of cloth which were sold in large numbers in America in 1920. This success prompted her to expand her sales to other Allied countries. In the summer of 1921, she travelled to Canada where she met with representatives of the Great War Veterans Association of Canada (which later became the Royal Canadian Legion). This body adopted the poppy as its national flower of Remembrance on 5 July 1921.

The big market, though, was closer at hand – across the Channel.

In that same year, a group of widows of French ex-servicemen crossed la Manche to visit Field Marshal Earl Haig. As Commander-in-Chief of the British Army, Haig had recently assisted in the creation of the Royal British Legion as a body to help ex-servicemen (it was officially formed on 15 May 1921). As in the USA, there was no direct Government support for those men incapacitated by the war at that time and many were either physically or emotionally unable to work. Even those capable of work experienced great difficulty in finding jobs during the years of high unemployment that followed the end of the war.

The French widows brought with them some of the poppies which they had made. They suggested that the poppies could be sold as a means of raising money for those ex-servicemen and women who had fallen on hard times. Haig accepted the proposal, and in the autumn of 1921, the British Legion formally adopted the Flanders poppy as its emblem. In the run-up to Remembrance Day that year the first British Legion Poppy Appeal was launched and proceeds from the sale of artificial French-made poppies were given to ex-servicemen in need of welfare and financial support.

'THE GREATEST FREE-WILL OFFERING IN THE WORLD'

Just as in the UK, so in Australia, where it was agreed that the Memorial Poppy would be worn on Remembrance Day 1921. The American and French Children's League sent a million artificial poppies to Australia for the Armistice Day commemoration that year. The Returned Soldiers and Sailors Imperial League sold poppies before 11 November, each costing one shilling. Of this amount, five pennies were donated to a French children's charity, six pennies were donated to the Returned Soldiers and Sailors Imperial League and one penny was received by the government.[4]

Some of Madame Guérin's representatives also went to New Zealand, meeting with the New Zealand Returned Soldiers' Association. The association agreed to purchase 350,000 small and 16,000 large French-made poppies from the French and American Children's League. Unfortunately, the shipment did not reach New Zealand in time for them to be promoted and sold before Remembrance Day. Instead, the first Poppy Day in New Zealand was on 24 April, the day before the annual ANZAC Day celebrations.

Also in 1922, a young British infantry officer called Major George Howson formed the Disabled Society to help ex-service personnel who had been disabled in the war. Howson approached the British Legion with the suggestion that the members of his society should be the people that manufactured the poppies, rather than buying them from the French. This led to the establishment of the Poppy Factory in Richmond later in 1922. The design of the poppies was kept simple so that even those people with severe disabilities could make them. Though the design has occasionally changed over time, the same simplicity of manufacture has been maintained. Dozens of disabled ex-service men and women still produce around 36,000,000 paper and plastic poppies at the factory each year.

According to Moina Michael, profits from 1921 to 1940 across the British Empire, including the Dominions, as obtained from statistics compiled by Earl Haig's British Legion Poppy programme, totalled £10,447,027. Haig proudly, and with some justification, called the Poppy Day Appeal, 'the greatest free-will offering in the world'.

A hundred years on, and many conflicts later, the poppy has become known across the world as the symbol of remembrance for those who lose their lives in war or are affected by it. Wreaths of poppies, cascading showers of poppies or the single stem, are worn, laid or dropped in their tens of thousands every November. At cemeteries or memorials in every continent the visitor is certain to see a splash of red amidst the pale gravestones – the same red that once covered those Flanders' fields. ●

NOTES
1. This account of the circumstances of Helmer's death has been compiled from letters received by Lieutenant Hague's father, from officers in the area at the time. They are quoted on the Canadian Great War Project, www.canadiangreatwarproject.com.
2. Moina Michael *The Miracle Flower, The Story of the Flanders Fields Memorial Poppy* (Dorrance and Company, Philadelphia, 1941), p.49.
3. For more information, please see: www.greatwar.co.uk/article/remembrance-poppy.
4. ibid.

THE KING'S PILGRIMAGE REMEMBERING THE FALLEN 1914-1918

THE KING'S PILGRIMAGE

In May 1922, King George V paid a personal tribute to the sacrifices of those who had given their lives in his name with a visit to the battlefields and memorials which had been the scenes of such terrible loss but also of great courage.

Many people, families and friends of those who had been killed in the war had crossed the Channel to see for themselves the places where their loved ones had fought and died. These were simple, personal affairs, and when King George decided that he too would undertake just such a pilgrimage, he wanted it to be also a personal affair, without the usual trappings of state which normally accompanied his official engagements.

The Royal Party was, correspondingly, a small one. The King would be accompanied at all times by Field-Marshal Earl Haig, who His Majesty had requested be at his side throughout. With them were three members of the Royal Suite and Major-General Sir Fabian Ware, the then Vice-Chairman of the Imperial War Graves Commission.

The pilgrimage began after the end of an official State visit to the King of the Belgians when, early on the morning of 11 May 1922, the Royal Train pulled out of Brussels station. Its destination was the port of Zeebrugge.

The first stop on the King's pilgrimage was the Churchyard in Zeebrugge, the last resting place of some of those who fell on the St. George's Day raid four years before. From there, the Royal Party went on to examine the scene of the exploits of HMS *Vindictive*, her supporting ships and the assaulting naval and Marine parties. It was a bright and breezy day as the King made his way along the infamous Mole, stopping at the point ➡

○ King George V examining wooden grave markers at an Imperial War Graves Commission Cemetery during his battlefield pilgrimage in May 1922.
(All images Historic Military Press)

REMEMBERING THE FALLEN 63

REMEMBERING THE FALLEN 1914-1918 THE KING'S PILGRIMAGE

King George V and his party make their way down the Mole at Zeebrugge on 11 May 1922.

where the submarine HMS *C3*, laden with high explosives, blew up, tearing a sixty-six-metre-wide gap. The positions where the blockships had been sunk were also noted, after which the Party moved on to inspect the very spot where the landing parties from *Vindictive* had scaled the Mole. In doing so, the King literally followed in the footsteps of Kaiser Wilhem II, who had undertaken an inspection at almost identical spots on 23 April 1918.

Returning to the Royal Train, the pilgrimage headed south to the station at Zonnebeke. That afternoon, having detrained, the Party was driven the short distance to Tyne Cot Cemetery. Despite having made many visits to the front during the First World War, this was the first time that the King had seen this cemetery.

Surrounded by the graves of so many of his subjects, the King turned to the large German pillbox which stood, somewhat battered, almost in the very middle of the cemetery. To those around him he remarked that 'it should never be moved' and 'should remain always as a monument to the heroes whose graves stood thickly around'.

His inspection of Tyne Cot was described by a reporter in the *Hull Daily Mail* the following day: 'Tyne Cot, with its 14,000 graves, is the largest of the British military cemeteries made by concentration since the war and its chief feature is the battered remnant of what was probably the first of the famous concrete bunker made by the Germans. The King went all over it and to the top of it, paying it special attention, because it is to be left as its stands as part of the memorial to the dead. Another object that attracted his attention was the grave of Sergeant McGee, the Australian VC. He also inspected the ex-service men who act as guardians of the cemetery.'

The King's route, after leaving Tyne Cot, brought him to the salient where the British Army had held the town of Ypres as the gate guarding the Channel ports. The royal party found the Cloth Hall still a ruin; the Cathedral more rubble than place of worship; and the old ramparts irrevocably damaged, scarred by the long years of war. But all around, the town was a hive of reconstruction – work which ground to a halt upon the realisation that the British King was in town.

The King was driven to the Menin Gate - that entry into and out of Ypres through which so many of Britain's young men had passed on their way to the trenches, never to return. But the view that lay before the King was not that which greets a visitor to the Menin Gate today – the famous memorial, with its great double arches enclosing an impressive vaulted hall, had yet to be built.

As the afternoon drew on, the Party headed out of Ypres for Vlamertinghe Military Cemetery, passing, but not stopping at, the British Cemetery behind Ypres Reservoir, the Asylum British Cemetery, another on the Dickebusch Road, and the Railway Château Cemetery. Having observed that so many of the British graves at Vlamertinghe were of Territorials, the King returned to his car.

The pilgrimage headed west away from Ypres along the road to Poperinghe. After some five-and-a-half kilometres, they reached Hop Store Cemetery. Hop Store village had been used from time to time as headquarters by both British artillery and field ambulance units.

Less than a mile further on and the Party reached Brandhoek – considered a relatively safe area during the war. Consequently, it provided an ideal location for field ambulances, each of which would, inevitably, be attended by the requisite graveyards. For this reason, there are three cemeteries at Brandhoek. The King visited the old, original, Military Cemetery.

TRIBUTE TO THE FRENCH

Back on the road, Poperinghe was next, following which was the large cemetery at Lijssenthoek. During the First World War, the village of Lijssenthoek had been situated on the main communication line between the Allied military bases in the rear and the Ypres battlefields. Close to the Front, but out of the extreme range of most German field artillery, it also became a natural place to establish casualty clearing stations. As well as being the second-largest Commonwealth cemetery on Belgian soil, it was also the last of the cemeteries in that country which the King and his entourage visited. From there, the border and the battlefields of France were but a short journey away.

The King crossed into France, by train, that evening, 11 May 1922. With the sun slowly setting, the Royal Train pulled into Hazebrouck station. After a meeting with local dignitaries, the train ploughed on, heading south to Vimy, which had been chosen as the resting place for the night, the King and his tiny entourage sleeping on the Royal Train.

Inspecting the British graves in Zeebrugge Churchyard. The memorial cross in the background is the Salvage Corps Memorial, whilst immediately behind the King are a number of German graves.

THE KING'S PILGRIMAGE REMEMBERING THE FALLEN 1914-1918

dominate the ridge for which the French fought a long and bloody battle. The ground was strategically important, and it became the focal point of three battles – the First, Second and Third Battles of Artois. They were battles that were as costly in French lives as the fighting around Verdun.

It was to there that the King came to pay his respects to the dead of the armies of France. In preparation, the King had personally written to Marshal Foch, asking if the great commander might meet him there. As a result, as the King walked up the steep slope of the hill of Notre Dame de Lorette, Foch was waiting to greet him.

○ The local name for the area of Tyne Cot Cemetery is Nieumolen, but British soldiers of the Northumberland Fusiliers, seeing on the German side of the line on Passchendaele Ridge a number of square shapes similar to the cottages back home on Tyneside, called the area Tyne Cot. In fact, the square shapes were newly-built concrete pillboxes. Inside the cemetery at Tyne Cot remain three of these structures – the largest one now has the Cross of Sacrifice on it. Here the King exits this large, central pillbox.

As the sun set, the King looked out on the shell-scarred fields of the ridge and, as one of the Party later wrote, 'bethought of the great battle in which his Canadian troops had won this key-position'.

The following morning, perhaps moved by the scenes surrounding him – the mine craters, shell holes and rambling trench systems, all still littered with the debris of war – the King requested that a telegram be sent to Lord Byng, the then Governor-General of Canada. In this, the King simply said: 'I have just spent the night at Vimy. My thoughts are with you.'

Within sight of Vimy Ridge was Notre Dame de Lorette. One of the major French national memorials and cemeteries, the chapel and tower at Notre Dame de Lorette

'In the course of my pilgrimage I have many times asked myself whether there can be more potent advocates of peace upon earth through the years to come than this massed multitude of silent witnesses to the desolation of war.'
King George V, May 1922

○ The King reads inscriptions on grave markers during his visit to the largest Commonwealth War Graves Cemetery in the world: Tyne Cot. It is located on the forward slope of the Passchendaele Ridge, and, as one of the Royal Party later wrote, 'no part of the long trench line which stretched from the sea to Switzerland has such shuddering memories for the British Army as Passchendaele'.

○ The Royal Party on the roof of the pillbox on which the Cross of Sacrifice at Tyne Cot stands today.

REMEMBERING THE FALLEN 1914-1918 **65**

REMEMBERING THE FALLEN 1914-1918 THE KING'S PILGRIMAGE

The Cross of Sacrifice in Tyne Cot Cemetery. Note the small section of the pillbox underneath, surrounded by a bronze wreath, that can be seen today.

en route such well-known places as Souchez and Mont St. Eloi. No break was taken at Arras and from there the King's journey continued on through Bapaume, Warlencourt and Le Sars. Crossing the tortured landscape of the Somme, the King stopped at as many of the cemeteries as time permitted: Warloy-Baillon, Forceville, Louvencourt, and Crouy were among their number. Intermittent rainstorms did not interfere with the programme, nor did they deter the local population who turned out to welcome the Royal Party at every turn.

As the Royal Party followed the straight road from Abbeville to Amiens, it came to the tiny village of Longpré-les-Corps Saints. Just beyond the village they stopped at the small cemetery that had taken the name of this community. This would be the King's last visit that day.

Having inspected the French Guard of Honour, the King and Foch slowly walked along the massed ranks of white wooden crosses in the cemetery. Reaching the memorial to the dead that had been erected at the top of the hill, the King turned to Foch. 'I am happy M. le Maréchal', he begun, 'that you are by my side at this moment, when I come to place this wreath in deserved homage to the heroic soldiers of France'. After laying a chaplet of red roses, upon which was the simple inscription 'From King George V, 12th May 1922', he then stood for a two-minute silence at the salute.

ON THE SOMME

Having taken its leave of Foch, the Royal Party headed by car to Albert, passing

That evening the King's train left Longpré and headed for the coast. The night was spent at Étaples; it would be early the next morning before the Royal Party arrived at Étaples Military Cemetery, the largest Commonwealth cemetery in France. Whilst at Étaples, the King had expressed the wish that he should meet representatives of the Dominions and visit, with them, the graves of their fellow countrymen. Accordingly, on entering the cemetery, the King was met by the High Commissioners for Canada, New Zealand, Newfoundland, and senior officers from Australia, India and South Africa. But before leaving, the King had one further act of homage to make.

In the weeks before the pilgrimage, one Mrs Jane Ellen Matthew had written to the Queen, 'as one mother to another', from her home in Devizes, Wiltshire. The events

The King lays a wreath during the visit to Notre Dame de Lorette.

The King saluting the French Colour Party at Notre Dame de Lorette on the second day of his tour.

THE KING'S PILGRIMAGE REMEMBERING THE FALLEN 1914-1918

The King visits the grave of Lieutenant Prince Maurice Victor Donald Battenberg in Ypres Town Cemetery (see page 16).

that followed were explained further in the *Taunton Courier and Western Advertiser* on 17 May: 'There was a little secret about those flowers which both Mr. and Mrs. Matthew had kept, as they thought, to themselves. One day it came out, and then the father and mother found that each of them had been associating a border of forget-me-nots in their garden with their dead boy, and the mother with an unspoken dream.

'The mother's dream was that some day a bunch of forget-me-nots from the old garden might be laid on the lad's grave in memory of his home and of those left behind. But the chance seemed as though it would never come. And then the mother heard that the King and Queen were to

At Étaples Cemetery the King is pictured here reading the letter written by Mrs. Jane Ellen Matthew.

go to Étaples Cemetery where the boy lay. Knowing nothing of Courts, and trusting only to a mother's instinct, Mrs. Matthew put a spray of forget-me-nots in a letter and sent it to the Queen, asking that they might be placed upon the grave.'

Aware that she would not be present with her husband at Étaples – she would arrive from Belgium later the same day – the Queen entrusted this task to her husband. Finding a suitable break in proceedings, the King produced Mrs Matthew's letter from his pocket. With the help of one of the gardeners, the King set off to locate the grave.

On reaching the last resting place of Serjeant DM2/178686 Alpheus Matthew, Royal Army Service Corps, the King dutifully bent down and placed upon the covering soil the mother's flowers. After a moment's silence, the King turned to those accompanying him and gave instructions

that 'special care should be taken of them, and that they were not on any account to be disturbed or removed'.

There then followed the last stages of the King's pilgrimage. From its high wind-swept cliff top location on the outskirts of Boulogne, Terlincthun British Cemetery stands sentinel over the English Channel. It was at Terlincthun that the only semblance of official ceremony was permitted by the King.

The citizens of Boulogne had assembled en masse around the cemetery where many relatives of the dead were gathered. In their presence, and that of numerous dignitaries, the King led a service of remembrance. In his message, the King went on to add: 'For

The King and Marshal Foch in discussion during the Royal Party's visit to Notre Dame de Lorette. Also known as Ablain St.-Nazaire French Military Cemetery, it is the world's largest French military cemetery.

The King spends a moment at the last resting place of Sergeant DM2/178686 Alpheus Matthew, Royal Army Service Corps, who died on 9 December 1918.

REMEMBERING THE FALLEN 67

REMEMBERING THE FALLEN 1914-1918 THE KING'S PILGRIMAGE

The Royal Party leaving Étaples, 13 May 1922.

the past few days I have been on a solemn pilgrimage in honour of a people who died for all free men … Standing beneath this Cross of Sacrifice, facing the great Stone of Remembrance, and compassed by these sternly simple headstones, we remember, and must charge our children to remember, that, as our dead were equal in sacrifice, so they are equal in honour, for the greatest and least of them have proved that sacrifice and honour are no vain things, but truths by which the world lives.'

The King's pilgrimage came to a close as buglers from the Coldstream and Grenadier Guards played the poignant notes of the Last Post.

As the Royal Navy warship carrying the King was escorted out of the harbour at Boulogne by a squadron of French destroyers, to rendezvous with a similar British squadron waiting out to sea, the King may well have found the time to reflect on the events of the last three days.

He might possibly have ruminated on his impromptu halt at Ypres Town Cemetery – a halt that he had requested at the last minute as his Party made its way into Ypres on the first day. It was there that a member of his own family, 23-year-old Lieutenant Prince Maurice Victor Donald Battenberg KCVO, Mentioned in Despatches, the youngest son of Prince Henry and Princess Beatrice of Battenberg and youngest grandson of Queen Victoria, was buried.

Like many other relatives across the years to come, the King was moved by the view of the cemetery that greeted him. The pages of the *Folkestone, Hythe, Sandgate & Cheriton Herald* of 20 May 1922, provides the following account: 'Ex-Pte. W. Parmentier, RAMC, a Folkestone man, who is employed by the Imperial War Graves Commission, was chosen by the Commission as their representative to escort the King around the Ypres Cemetery. Mr. Parmentier, who has been employed by the Commission for three years, was congratulated by His Majesty on the care that he had taken with the grave of Prince Maurice of Battenberg.'

Standing looking at the Prince's grave, marked by a large wooden cross, the King may have well have found himself experiencing the same emotions and feelings as so many of his subjects around the world – the grief, sadness and emptiness at the loss of a loved one who made the ultimate sacrifice in the service of King and Country.

One of the last stops on the third day of the tour was Crouy British Cemetery, where the King took a moment to talk to two bereaved Australian relatives. About eleven miles north-west of Amiens on the west side of the River Somme, on the Amiens-Abbeville main road, the cemetery was used between April and August 1918 for burials from the 5th and 47th Casualty Clearing Stations, which had come to the village because of the German advance.

The King lays a wreath at the base of the Cross of Sacrifice in Terlincthun British Cemetery.

68 REMEMBERING THE FALLEN

THE MENIN GATE REMEMBERING THE FALLEN 1914-1918

THE MENIN GATE

Before the outbreak of war, the Menin Gate was a crossing point over the moat and through the ramparts that ringed the Belgian city of Ypres. During the bitter fighting in the Salient it was one of the main routes used by Allied troops to reach the front.

How best to remember the fallen of the Great War was a much-discussed subject in the months that followed the Armistice. Graves, collected in cemeteries, were already being developed or their sites selected, and structures planned. But what of the missing, of whom there were an estimated 300,000? If monuments of some description were to be created to honour the missing, what form should they take and where should they be sited? If any such memorials were to be erected in one of the cemeteries close to where it was believed the individuals had died, then their construction would affect the plans already in place for the cemeteries.

The bodies who had to wrestle with this problem were the Imperial War Graves Commission and the British Department of Works. Lieutenant Colonel F.R. Durham, the Director of Works, came up with an idea that would ensure the names of the missing were permanently recorded in the relevant cemeteries without the added

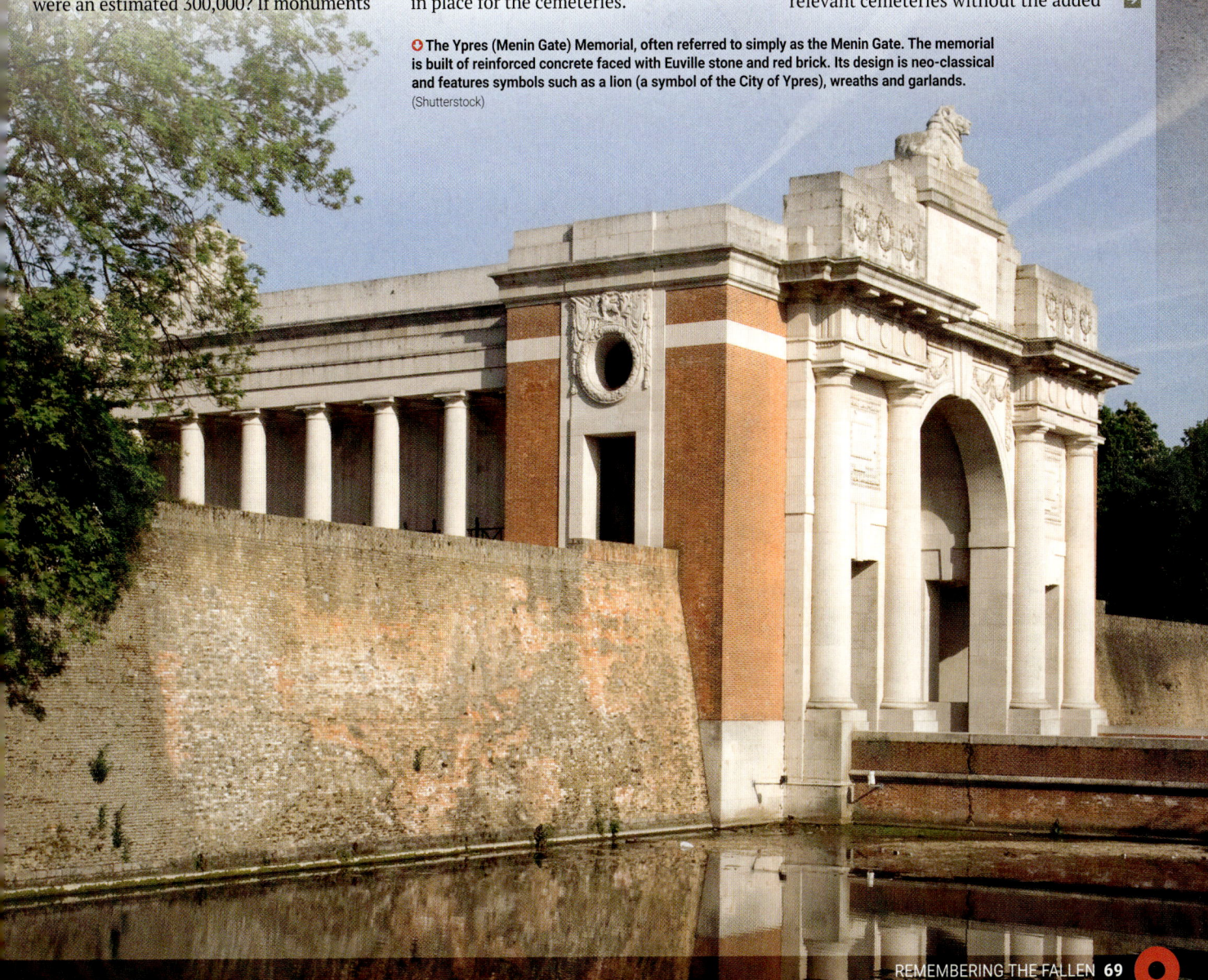

◉ The Ypres (Menin Gate) Memorial, often referred to simply as the Menin Gate. The memorial is built of reinforced concrete faced with Euville stone and red brick. Its design is neo-classical and features symbols such as a lion (a symbol of the City of Ypres), wreaths and garlands.
(Shutterstock)

REMEMBERING THE FALLEN 1914-1918 THE MENIN GATE

○ Field Marshal Lord Plumer at the unveiling of the Menin Gate Memorial, 24 July 1927. (University of Victoria Libraries, Canada)

○ The moat by the Menin gate pictured in April or May 1919. The Memorial was built to the photographer's right. (Department of National Defence/Library and Archives Canada)

cost and redrawing of the existing plans, by putting the names of the missing in the cemetery record book in the record houses where each grave was listed. Durham also suggested an even simpler alternative, which was to have one record house built for each regiment or unit that would act as a commemorative chapel, and the names of the missing could be inscribed on its walls. That would have the added benefit of saving the IWGC the time-consuming task of trying to discover where each man had been killed. The names of the missing could be easily extracted from the regimental records. The geographical principle could be satisfied by placing the record houses at places along the front most closely associated with each regiment.

While Colonel Durham's plans were inexpensive, simple and easily put in place, there were objections by people who saw this as being too impersonal. To an individual soldier, his regiment meant little, in that the majority of the missing were not professional soldiers but civilians formed into temporary battalions of which most regiments had a dozen or more. The place where they were killed, on the other hand, was uniquely important to that individual. However, Lieutenant Colonel H.F. Chettle, the Director of Records, pointed out that trying to track down the last known place of all the missing meant the date of each man's death would have to be ascertained, and that this process would probably take up to five years.

The IWGC could not make up its mind, so, in typical British fashion, it set up a committee. Also, in true British style, it was recognised that some form of compromise would, in the end, have to be made. Eventually, it was agreed that 'the commemoration of the missing near the place of death would be satisfied by attributing a cemetery or certain cemeteries within the area of such action to each of the considerable actions on the Western Front.' What this meant was, that instead of allocating the names to some 300 cemeteries, they would be grouped in eighty-five cemeteries corresponding to those main battle areas as defined in the report of the Battles Nomenclature Committee which had already been set up by the British Government. This plan was soon rejected when the Commission became involved in yet another thorny question – that of national war memorials. Its answer to that was to involve another committee, or, in fact, two committees.

THE BATTLE EXPLOITS MEMORIAL COMMITTEE

The Imperial War Graves Commission originally had a straightforward objective, even if the means of achieving that

○ A view of the area of the Menin Gate, looking into the shattered ruins of the city of Ypres, taken in April or May 1919. (Department of National Defence/Library and Archives Canada)

MENIN GATE REMEMBERING THE FALLEN 1914-1918

IMPERIAL WAR GRAVES COMMISSION

ORDER OF CEREMONIAL
AT THE UNVEILING AND DEDICATION
OF THE MEMORIAL
AT THE
MENIN GATE, YPRES
BY FIELD-MARSHAL LORD PLUMER
G.C.B., G.C.M.G., G.C.V.O., G.B.E.
ON
SUNDAY, JULY 24th, 1927
AT 10.30 A.M.

THIS MEMORIAL IS ERECTED BY THE IMPERIAL WAR GRAVES COMMISSION IN HONOUR OF THE BRITISH ARMIES WHO STOOD AT YPRES FROM 1914 TO 1918, AND OF 56,000 OF THOSE OF THEIR DEAD WHO FELL IN THE SALIENT AND WHO HAVE NO KNOWN GRAVE

○ As this programme states, the Ypres (Menin Gate) Memorial, designed by Sir Reginald Blomfield, was unveiled by Field Marshal Lord Plumer on 24 July 1927. (Historic Military Press)

○ The central hall is dominated by the name panels of the missing which run along the entire length of the interior. The name panels are inset into the stonework of the interior, slightly recessed from the surface. The panels are formed of stone slabs into which the names have been inscribed. (Shutterstock)

objective were complex – to record the graves of individual warriors and provide them with a fitting burial in suitable cemeteries. National memorials were not part of its remit, but as increasing numbers of people from the Dominions and India voiced their desire to see such monuments, there was no other body with the knowledge and resources to create these memorials. This was especially the case with the building of any such memorials in France, for the IWGC was the only body which the French Government would deal with concerning requests for permission to erect memorials on its land. The IWGC, therefore, had to become involved in the construction of national memorials, though it handed responsibility for choosing between the competing claims to the Battle Exploits Memorial Committee and the Historical Section of the Committee of Imperial Defence.

There was also a strong desire for regiments and corps to erect monuments to the sacrifices of its men. Some of the wealthier of these regiments were willing to spend considerable sums on memorials. This seemed wholly unjust, as those who had lost their lives had all done so for the same cause. So, the idea grew of creating a few large memorials, giving equal credit to all involved, would be preferable to a multitude of smaller memorials scattered across the whole of the Western Front. This suggestion was given greater force when it was learned that some of the countries of the Empire had decided to hand out public funds for the creation of memorials to commemorate the battle exploits of their troops. Parsimonious or not, the British Government could not be the only one not to pay tribute to the deeds of its warriors.

It was Winston Churchill who persuaded the Cabinet, in January 1919, that it was the country's duty to create lasting memorials to the fighting men of its nation. His idea was for several general memorials to be erected on the principal battlefields of the war, at Ypres, Mons, Arras, the Somme, the Hindenburg Line, Gallipoli and Jerusalem.

The basic principle of government-funded memorials was accepted but, of course, the final decision on the nature and location of such memorials had to be governed by – a committee! This particular one was called the National Battlefield Memorials Committee, and amongst its members were Dominion High Commissioners. Its remit was to report on 'the forms of National War Memorials and the sites on which they should be erected, together with estimates of costs'.[1]

THE YPRES SALIENT

Churchill was amongst those who favoured a great national monument at Ypres. Along with the Somme, the fighting at Ypres had been the deadliest of the war for the British and Empire troops. But, unlike the chalky, well-drained, soil of the Somme, the men had to live and fight in and around Ypres amid a morass of Flanders mud. Though the significance and sacrifice of the Battle of the Somme had not been forgotten, it was the scenes of waterlogged trenches, of troops trudging through knee-deep mud which covered their harrowed, unwashed faces, that came to epitomise in so many people's minds, the squalid, inglorious conditions in which the war had been fought. It was also where a quarter of a million British and Empire soldiers lay dead.

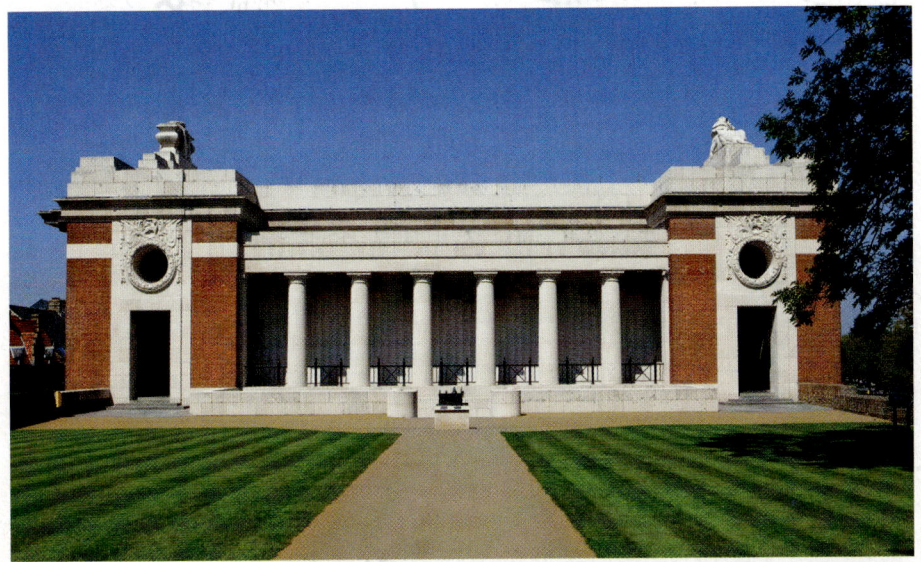

○ The south face of the Menin Gate. Its designer, Sir Reginald Blomfield, sought to design a fitting memorial based around the concept of a triumphal arch and a central hall. He drew inspiration from the seventeenth century Porte de la Citadelle in Nancy, France, a structure he admired. (Shutterstock)

REMEMBERING THE FALLEN 71

REMEMBERING THE FALLEN 1914-1918 THE MENIN GATE

Every evening since 1928, at 20.00 hours, buglers sound the Last Post at the Menin Gate. The ceremony has become part of the daily life of Ypres and traffic is stopped from passing through the memorial. Only during the German occupation in the Second World War was the ceremony interrupted, during which period it was held at Brookwood Military Cemetery in Surrey. The idea of performing the Last Post was first conceived by the Superintendent of the local police force, Pierre Vandenbraambussche. (Trabantos/Shutterstock)

One of the 54,608 casualties named on the Ypres (Menin Gate) Memorial. Private Thomas William Fleming, 1st Battalion Royal Irish Regiment, was killed in action near Hooge on 7 May 1915. He was 24 years old. His name can be found on Panel 33. (Courtesy of Gerard Fleming; Europeana14-18)

In January 1919, just months after the Armistice, Ypres was still in ruins and it was these crumbled buildings that had once been part of a bustling, prosperous, Flemish city, that inspired Churchill to declare the following: 'I should like us to acquire the whole of the ruins of Ypres ... A more sacred place for the British race does not exist in the world.' Like so many of Churchill's more extravagant ideas, such a proposition was entirely impracticable, for Ypres was the home of thousands of people and had to be rebuilt, as had their lives, families and businesses. Indeed, it was the most important city in the area – it could not simply be handed over to the British to preserve as a ruin. On the other hand, the Belgian Government was not adverse to the creation of some great monument, and, in fact, such a scheme might help in the reconstruction of the city and provide much-needed local jobs.

Others had almost equally grand ideas of 'one great and sacred repository of all the shattered dead in the [Ypres] Salient ... A great marble chapel and sanctuary' being built opposite the city's famous Cloth Hall. 'The cemeteries of the first Seven Divisions [of the British Army] would range along the streets by the eastern Menin Gate whose cobblestones are worn by the tramp during those four years of our infantry and the restless wheels of our guns.'[2] What the Ypres authorities decided to do, was leave the Cloth Hall, the old Menin Gate and the severely damaged ramparts in their ruined state until the British decided what they were going to do. This enabled the local authorities to concentrate on rebuilding the houses and shops so essential to the citizens.

THE MENIN GATE

As the Belgians were willing to leave the above-named sites in Ypres to the British to reconstruct how they saw fit, it paved the way for the British Government to commit to making Ypres the site of its first great national monument. The distinguished architect Sir Reginald Bloomfield was instructed to travel to Ypres and make his recommendations. He duly set off for Belgium in September 1919.

In the interim, the Belgians had withdrawn their offer of the Cloth Hall, which they instead decided to rebuild exactly as it was before the war. This left just the Menin Gate and the Vaubanesque ramparts. The choice was obvious. A great number of those soldiers who had fought in the great battles in the Ypres Salient, including those who were still missing, had at some point, passed through the Menin Gate. There could scarcely be a more fitting place for a monument to those men with no known grave.

Bloomfield's plans were laid before the Cabinet and approved, along with a grant of £150,000. This monument would be an, 'Imperial Memorial in the form of a gateway

A brass model of the Menin Gate that can be seen up on the ramparts beside the Memorial. The Menin Gate commemorates casualties from the forces of Australia, Canada, India, South Africa and the United Kingdom who died in the Salient. In the case of casualties from the United Kingdom, only those who died prior 16 August 1917 (with some exceptions) are commemorated. United Kingdom and New Zealand servicemen who died after that date are named on the memorial at Tyne Cot, a site which marks the furthest point reached by Commonwealth forces in Belgium until nearly the end of the war. New Zealand casualties who died prior to 16 August 1917 are commemorated on memorials at Buttes New British Cemetery and Messines Ridge British Cemetery. (Historic Military Press)

THE MENIN GATE REMEMBERING THE FALLEN 1914-1918

at the Menin Gate'. At the same time, money was also earmarked for other memorials at important battlefields.

Work began on the new structure in June 1923. Meanwhile, the vital task collecting all the names of the missing which would be inscribed upon what would be a magnificent structure had already begun, though at this stage it was not known exactly how many individuals there would be. Their names, once they had been compiled on the appropriate lists, would be inscribed on stone panels which could be fixed in place once the structure was complete. This meant that the construction programme could continue uninterrupted.

As it transpired, the Ypres (Menin Gate) Memorial's 1,200 panels could only accommodate some 60,000 names which, it soon became evident, was far short of the total number of missing in that region. It was therefore decided that those who fell after the Battle of Messines in 1917 would be placed on another memorial at Tyne Cot and later at Armentières. Eventually, the great monument was completed in 1927 and its inauguration was planned for 24 July.

THE LAST POST

When the Menin Gate Memorial to the Missing was unveiled on 24 July 1927, on what was a brilliantly sunny day, the ceremony was attended by Albert, King of the Belgians, Field Marshal Lord Plumer and General Foch of France. Hundreds of local inhabitants, veterans of 1914-1918 and relatives of the fallen British and Commonwealth troops, were gathered in the Grand Place and along the route to the Menin Gate.

○ The Menin Gate is one of four memorials to the missing in Belgian Flanders, which cover the area known as the Ypres Salient. The memorial seen here, the Ploegsteert Memorial, is not one of these, but its proximity to Ypres means that many visitors to the Ypres Salient include it in their itinerary. The Ploegsteert Memorial, which stands in Berks Cemetery Extension south of Ypres, is pictured here being unveiled by the Duke of Brabant on 7 June 1931. This memorial commemorates the missing of the Lys battlefield sector. (Historic Military Press)

Tens of thousands were standing on the ramparts either side of the memorial and along the road opposite the memorial on the eastern side of the moat. Several hundred veterans and relatives were crowded into the street leading to the memorial from the Menin Road. Individuals were in every open window of the newly built houses overlooking the memorial. Press photographers stood on walls or ladders to get a good vantage point. Loudspeakers were set up to enable everyone to hear the ceremony, even in the Grande Place. Millions were also listening to the ceremony which was broadcast on the wireless in Britain.

Ever since that memorable day in 1927, apart from a brief period during the Second World War, crowds flock to the Menin Gate to watch the ceremony which takes place every evening at 20.00 hours. The climax of that ceremony is the sounding of the Last Post, the memory of which is never forgotten by those who have the good fortune to experience it. ●

NOTES
1. Philip Longworth, *The Unending Vigil, The History of the Commonwealth War Graves Commission* (Pen & Sword, Barnsley, 2010), pp.85-6.
2. Henry Becles Wilson, *Ypres, The Holy Ground of British Arms* (Batsford, 1920), p.xiii.

○ Another of the Great War memorials, the Loos Memorial, being dedicated by Sir Nevil Macready on 4 August 1930. The Loos Memorial commemorates over 20,000 officers and men who fell in the area from the River Lys to the old southern boundary of the First Army, from the first day of the Battle of Loos to the end of the war, and who have no known grave. The Memorial forms the sides and back of Dud Corner Cemetery. (National Library of France)

GREAT SUBSCRIPTION OFFERS FROM KEY

SUBSCRIBE
TO *YOUR* FAVOURITE MAGAZINE
AND SAVE

Remembering the Fallen

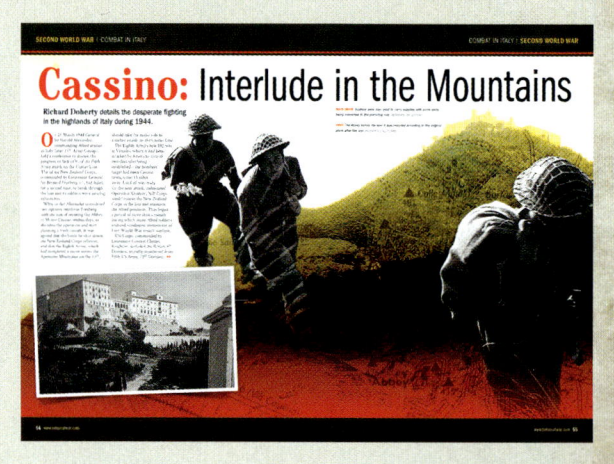

The UKs best-selling Military History Title

Britain at War is dedicated to exploring every aspect of Britain's involvement in conflicts from the turn of the 20th century through to modern day. From World War I to the Falklands, World War II to Iraq, readers are able to re-live decisive moments in Britain's history through fascinating insight combined with rare and previously unseen photography.

www.britainatwar.com

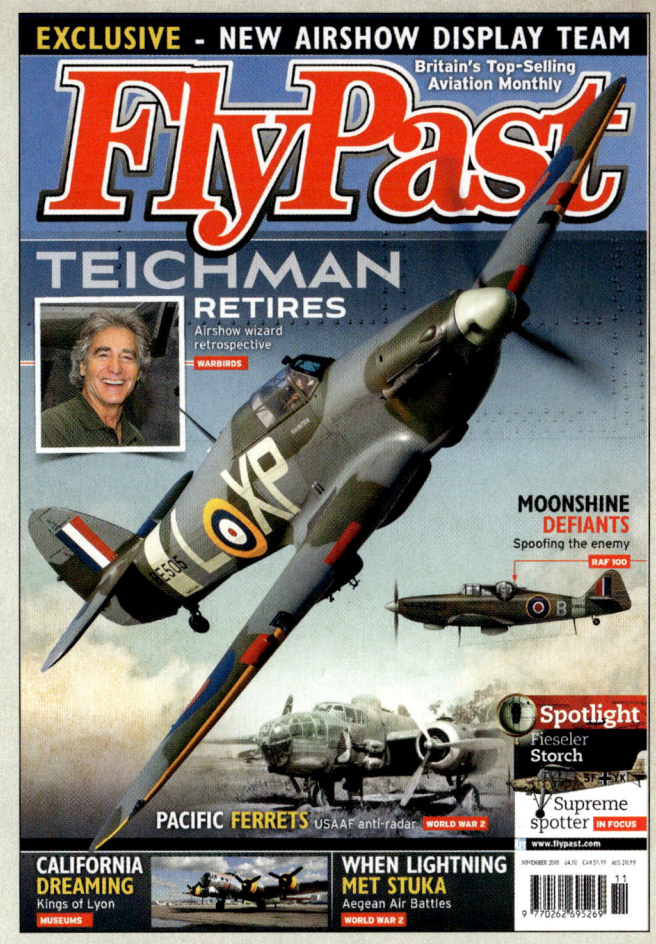

History in the Air Since 1911

Aeroplane traces its lineage back to the weekly The Aeroplane launched in June 1911, and is still continuing to provide the best aviation coverage around. **Aeroplane** magazine is dedicated to offering the most in-depth and entertaining read on all historical aircraft.

www.aeroplanemonthly.com

Britain's Top-Selling Aviation Monthly

Having pioneered coverage of this fascinating world of 'living history' since 1980, **FlyPast** still leads the field today. Subjects regularly profiled include British and American aircraft type histories, as well as those of squadrons and units from World War One to the Cold War.

www.flypast.com

ALSO AVAILABLE DIGITALLY:

Available on iTunes • Available on the App Store • Available on Google play • Available on kindle fire • Available on PC, Mac & Windows 10

Available on PC, Mac and Windows 10 from pocketmags.com

900/18

FOR THE LATEST SUBSCRIPTION DEALS

VISIT: www.keypublishing.com/shop

PHONE: (UK) 01780 480404   (Overseas) +44 1780 480404

REMEMBERING THE FALLEN 1914-1918 THE BATTLEFIELD TOURISTS

THE BATTLEFIELD TOURISTS

A hundred years earlier the battlefield of Waterloo had become a major tourist attraction, but only for the wealthier classes. In the more equitable twentieth century, the battlefields of the First World War were accessible to many more people, and battlefield tourism began to flourish on an unprecedented scale.

After the first waves of grief had washed over the Allied nations, many people sought to visit the places where their loved ones had perished, and others, perhaps fascinated and intrigued by the climatic events which had shaped their lives for four gruelling years, wished to see where the momentous battles had been fought – some won, some lost.

Such was the demand from ordinary working people to visit the battlefields, the St. Barnabas Society was founded in 1919 by a New Zealand padre, the Reverend H. Mullineux, to assist the bereaved with their wish to visit the graves of their loved ones. The society organized group trips, which cost less than an individual excursion, enabling many poorer families to undertake journeys that would otherwise be beyond their financial means. In France from 1921 onwards, free trips were organized annually by the St. Barnabas Society for the relatives of deceased soldiers.

Others, less philanthropically, also saw the opportunity to make money out of this burgeoning demand, and tours of the battlefields, led by tour guides, were

◯ A visitor to the Ypres Salient poses for the camera by what appears to be a German 21cm Mörser m/10-16 heavy howitzer on display in the centre of Ypres at the time of his tour. Note the vehicles in the background – all of which were typical of those used during battlefield tours of the Salient.
(All images Historic Military Press unless stated otherwise)

THE BATTLEFIELD TOURISTS REMEMBERING THE FALLEN 1914-1918

○ A group of veterans pictured during a visit to the Ypres Salient during the 1920s or 1930s. Information that accompanies the album that this picture is taken from suggests that the members of the party came from Yorkshire.

lost their lives in the places described. An excerpt from the Marne guide exemplifies this well: 'Ruins are more impressive when coupled with a knowledge of their origin and destruction. A stretch of country which might seem dull and uninteresting to the unenlightened eye becomes transformed at the thought of the battles that have raged there. The wealth of illustrations and authentic map ... offer the prospective tourist a most interesting study, preliminary to a very instructive and delightful journey beneath the sunny skies of France.' A delightful journey was hardly what bereaved families thought of the pilgrimages they had undertaken.

Other companies sought to take advantage of these new lucrative business opportunities, including railway companies which, as early as 1920, offered 'Weekend Tours of the Battlefields of Belgium' for created by the likes of Thomas Cook and the French company Michelin. The original Michelin guide books were designed to encourage the owners of the relatively few motors cars that then existed to drive more, and thus enable Michelin to sell more tyres (adverts for which were, of course, featured in the books). Over time, the Michelin Battlefield Guides became hugely successful in their own right, selling 2 million copies in forty-six different languages between 1919 and 1938.

The tone of the Michelin guides evoked disapproval from some quarters, for not showing due respect for those who had

○ This was the bus that the members of the party from Yorkshire used to travel around various sites in the Ypres Salient. The bus was operated by a company based in **Poperinghe**.

just £8. Pilgrims, making their trips to the battlefields and cemeteries, continued to complain that the new breed of tourists failed to show due respect when visiting such sacred places. That is because these tours were not sorrowful sojourns for the bereaved, they were for those interested in the spectacle that the battlefields, the wrecks, abandoned ordnance, trenches and the tortured, cratered landscape, presented. While the big towns such as Ypres or Péronne were feverish hives of activity, many of the buildings and roads were still piles of rubble. The situation out in the countryside was often worse, many of those villagers who had returned living in wooden shacks or hastily erected Nissen huts. Some were even reduced to camping amongst the debris of their former homes.

○ Scattered relics and ordnance near the Menin Road that the veterans from Yorkshire encountered during their tour.

REMEMBERING THE FALLEN 77

REMEMBERING THE FALLEN 1914-1918 THE BATTLEFIELD TOURISTS

◯ The Yorkshiremen's tour of the Salient suffers a glitch as their coach appears to have slipped off the road into a ditch.

◯ Battlefield relics and preserved trenches, labelled as off the Menin Road, photographed during the tour by the Yorkshire-based veterans. Note the assorted rifles to the left of the trench.

Nevertheless, from amidst the ruins, the locals sought to take advantage of the tourist phenomenon. 'There was a ruthless gaiety about it,' stated one account. 'Picturesque postcards of the battlefields were sold along with "authentic" souvenirs ... Bluffs of rusting shells and hills of scrap metal rose beside the craters, tough men grinning beside them. As for the human waste – the early impromptu cemeteries were often mongrel affairs: German, French, British. It took years to shuffle them into their scared national corners.

◯ The original caption to this, the last of our set of pictures depicting the tour undertaken by the veterans from Yorkshire, states that they are 'examining battlefield relics such as bomb throwers, possibly near the Menin Road'.

◯ The original caption to this image states that it shows visitors inspecting a German howitzer near the Cloth Hall. It adds that at the time the image was taken, 'excavations are being made under the building to recover the bodies of soldiers killed by gas. The ground is so impregnated with poisonous fumes that operations frequently have to be suspended.'

'The landscape was still dangerous ... the lovely churches in ruins (and the ruins themselves falling down), the trees skeletal. Local children, eager to earn a few francs, hunted for metal bits or brought in shells. People were killed and maimed hoeing their cabbages, or picking dandelions, or ploughing their fields.'[1]

It was against this backdrop that those early visitors made their way to the Western Front. For an individual tourist, locations such as Ypres were relatively easy to get to. The traveller could leave Victoria Station in London at 08.45 hours in the morning, for example, and be at Ypres by 20.17 hours that evening – all for the cost of £1 2s 11d for a single ticket. Once there, there would be no shortage of entrepreneurs anxious to help at a price. For example, half a mile down the Dickebush road a former British officer ran a recommended garage and hired out cars at two francs per kilometre.[2]

By 1920, official bodies and large organisations were playing a part in the battlefield tour business, in some cases the intention being to safeguard the best interests of the traveller. The YMCA, for example, soon introduced an organised tour of the Somme that cost £6. Organisations like the Church Army, the British Legion, Red Cross and Ypres League followed suit.

○ An early battlefield tour guide for the Somme – in this case one of the famous series by Michelin which was first published in 1919.

○ Another early battlefield guide, in this case a 'Touring Atlas of the Western Battlefields' produced by the White Cross Insurance Association for the benefit of its policy holders.

THE GALLIPOLI OAK

It was not only in France and Belgium that British and Empire troops had fought during the First World War. Gallipoli and the Dardanelles had also seen some of the deadliest fighting, the most difficult and dangerous conditions. But Turkey is a long way from the UK and no tours of the kind offered by Mr Thomas Cook were available to those who wished to see where their loved ones had perished. That, though, would not stop one man, whose journey to Gallipoli has left a lasting legacy, and whose determination epitomises the endeavours of so many to visit the places so sacred to themselves and their families.

It was in March 1922, that a 58-year-old businessman from Rochdale in Lancashire stepped ashore at Gallipoli, where his eldest son, Lieutenant Eric Duckworth, had died. James Duckworth and his wife had joined a ship at Marseilles for a cruise around the Mediterranean, the itinerary of which included passing close by the **Dardanelles** Strait. It was for that reason Mr and Mrs Duckworth were onboard the cruise ship, as, it seems, were many others. It is not known whether or not the people on the ship had planned their action together, or that it was the unconnected efforts of numerous individuals, but the combined appeals of the passengers persuaded the owners of the ship to dock for two days on the western side of the Gallipoli Peninsula.

At first, though, things did not go well, as James Duckworth recalled:

'Unfortunately, a rough sea got up in the night which rendered any landing outside the straits quite impossible. We therefore entered the Dardanelles [on the eastern or opposite side of the peninsula] and at midnight one began to fear the main object of the trip would have to be cancelled.'

The weather, and the Duckworth's fortunes, began to improve. 'In the early morning we hove to at Chanak [a large town on the Turkish mainland] and after clearing quarantine and other formalities proceeded across the straits and dropped anchor in Khalia Bay, where is the GHQ of the International War Graves Commission. What had originally threatened to be a misfortune turned out entirely in our favour.'[3]

What proved so favourable for James Duckworth was that the place where the ship had anchored was where the man who might be able to direct him to the scene of his son's last known movements, Colonel Hughes of the War Graves Commission, had his headquarters. Duckworth and the other passengers from the cruise ship were not the first visitors Hughes had welcomed, but there had been nothing on the scale of the large party which descended upon him that morning. As with so many of the French and Belgium battlefields, the Gallipoli Peninsula was still a dangerous place, with much unrecovered ordnance still lying around, and dug-outs and trenches to trip the uncautious visitor.

On that first day of their visit, Hughes took the party around the sectors held mostly by the men of the Australian

○ The group of officers, NCOs and cadets from the Territorial Cadet Force on the cross-Channel ferry *Pieter de Conincke* having sailed from Dover bound for Ostend, 30 July 1925.

○ A handwritten comment on the rear of this image indicates that it shows a lady during a visit to the Ypres Salient soon after the end of the First World War. Note the tour vehicles and stands in the middle distance, all linked to the growing trade in battlefield tourism. The ruins of the Cloth Hall, being rebuilt at the time, can be seen in the background.

REMEMBERING THE FALLEN 79

REMEMBERING THE FALLEN 1914-1918 THE BATTLEF

↻ During their visit to Zeebrugge and Ostend, the Territorial Cadet Force members' itinerary included a visit to this coastal gun emplacement – which shows signs of having been damaged at some point. This is possibly the Long Max gun that was positioned at Moere, about eight miles from Ostend.

Armed, then, with much important information, on day two of the visit, the Duckworths were able to make their way, with Colonel Hughes' help, to a certain place shown on the sketch. 'The lines of trenches, apart from the effects of wind and weather, remain as they were left over six years ago, except where places have been filled in to admit cross of traffic,' noted James Duckworth. 'The ground has been well cleared of wire, equipment, spent cartridges and shell cases.' But the Duckworths intended to do more than just visit the place where Eric had been killed, and whose body had not been identified.

Mr Duckworth had taken with him a sapling and an inscribed stone to plant and lay where his son had died. Realising that such items would soon be forgotten or lost in so remote a spot, James Duckworth decided that the best place for them would be in the nearby Redoubt Cemetery at Helles where so many of his former friends lay. That oak tree still flourishes today, to be wondered and admired by the battlefield tourists of the twenty-first century.

A FAMILY'S VISIT

Hundreds of thousands flooded across the Channel in the inter-war years to see the former battlefields and an incredible 50,000 watched the unveiling of the Menin Gate in 1928. Indeed, by the time that the family of one casualty, 27-year-old Private Norman Griffiths, made their pilgrimage to the Western Front in 1930, the battlefield tour was a well-established aspect of daily life in those parts of France and Belgium that had been touched by the war.

and New Zealand Army Corps, the ANZACs. This was a frustrating day for the Duckworths who had brought with them a sketch map which had been given to them by surviving comrades of Eric from the 6th Battalion Lancashire Fusiliers, in the hope that they could pinpoint the precise place where their son had last been seen alive. Indeed, the battalion's chaplain had assured them that, 'There will be no difficulty at all in describing to you the exact spot where the lad fell. Many know the spot.'

BATTLEFIELD TOURS

THE CARIBOU NEWFOUNDLAND MEMORIAL PARK

ONE DAY TOUR OF THE SOMME AND ANCRE BATTLEFIELDS BY PRIVATE CAR

PICKFORDS LD.
21/24 Cockspur Street, London, S.W.1
Société Anonyme Pickfords,
12 Rue Port Mahon, Paris

↻↻ Produced during the 1920s, this brochure promoted a tour of the Somme and Ancre battlefield, by private car, organised and sold by Pickfords Ltd.

A dairyman from Bilston in Staffordshire, Norman Griffiths had enlisted on 11 December 1916. A short, stocky individual, he was posted to No.1 Depot Royal Field Artillery at Newcastle on Tyne. On 26 September 1916, he sailed from Dover for France, soon finding himself at a base camp at Étaples.

↻ A description of the events of St George's Day, 1918 is provided to the party from the Territorial Cadet Force as they stand on the Mole at Zeebrugge.

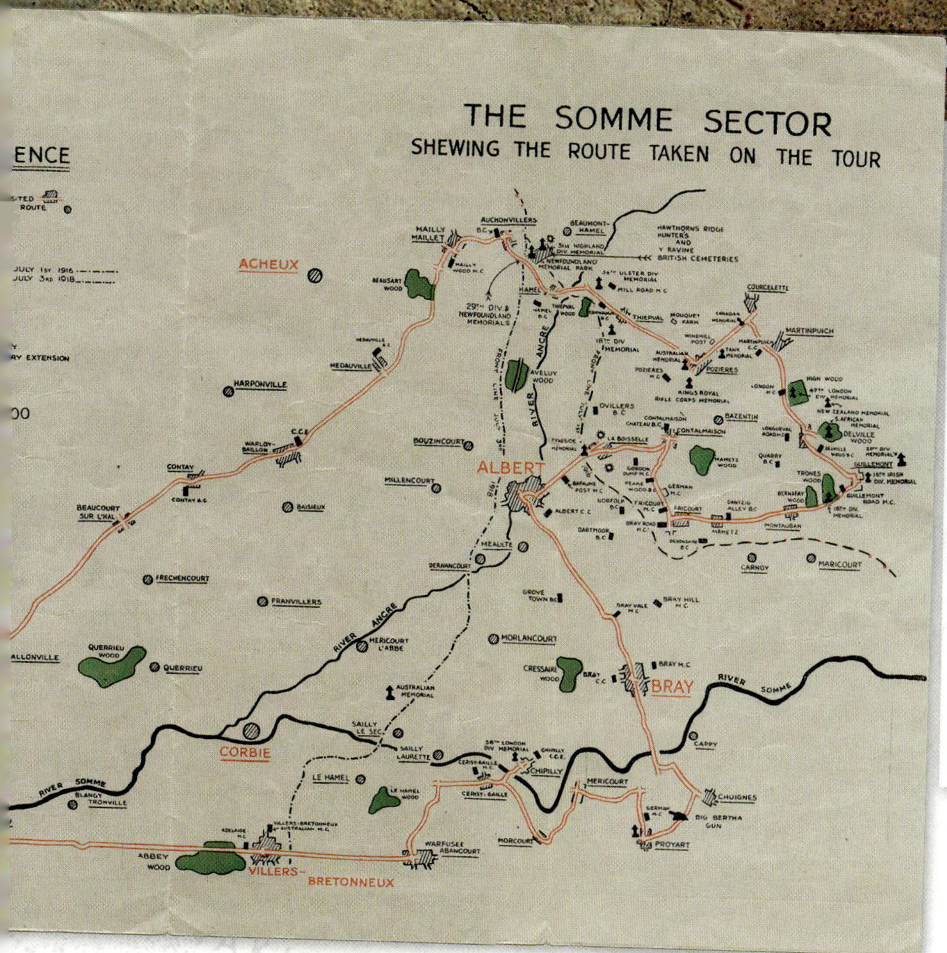

THE SOMME SECTOR
SHEWING THE ROUTE TAKEN ON THE TOUR

G THE FALLEN 1914-1918

◯ Norman Griffiths' sister pictured in front of his grave in Abbeville Communal Cemetery Extension during a family pilgrimage to France and Belgium in August 1930.

◯ A relative pictured beside Norman Griffiths' standard Imperial (later Commonwealth) War Graves Commission headstone.

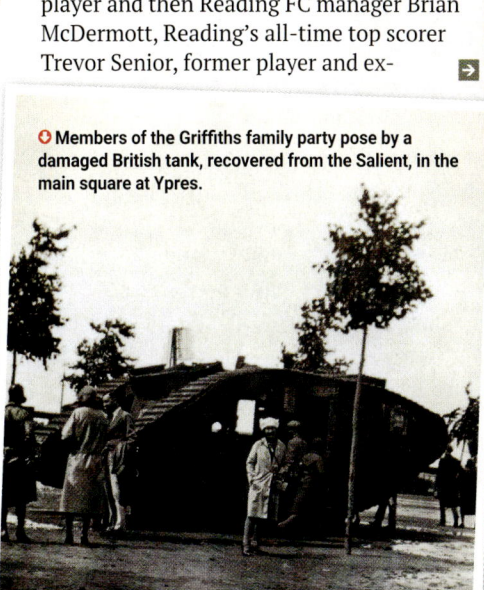

◯ Members of the Griffiths family party pose by a damaged British tank, recovered from the Salient, in the main square at Ypres.

As his training continued, Norman was transferred to the infantry, joining the 8th Battalion Duke of Wellington's (West Riding Regiment) on 13 October 1916. Within weeks of his arrival, however, conditions at the front soon began to take their toll on his health. On 9 December 1916, Norman was admitted to No.49 Casualty Clearing Station suffering from trench foot and tonsillitis.

On 21 January the following year Norman re-joined his unit. His return, though, was short-lived for he was taken ill again five days later. Passed up through the casualty evacuation chain, he arrived at No.2 Stationary Hospital at Abbeville later the same day. As the hours passed, his condition worsened until, at 17.00 hours on 31 January 1917, he passed away. His Army Form B.103, the 'Casualty Form – Active Service', notes that he died of Bronco-Pneumonia. He was duly buried in Abbeville Communal Cemetery Extension.

During their journey through the landscape that had been the Western Front, Norman's family visited sites such as Hill 60, the Cloth Hall in Ypres, Tyne Cot and so on – locations that have remained on the itineraries of battlefield tours ever since, and will, no doubt, remain so into the future. Their visit to plot II.A.24. of Abbeville Communal Cemetery Extension, however, was a very private and poignant one. After all, this was a family's personal pilgrimage to the last resting place of one of its own.

ON THE SOMME
Over the succeeding years, tours of a somewhat different natured developed. These were tours organized by military and naval bodies and were of an instructional, rather than a voyeuristic nature. Such tours were conducted at a course, unit, or even staff college level. They might be for the lowest ranks or the highest, for the newest recruit (some tours were part of basic training) or the most experienced.

The aims may also vary. For example, a tour's purpose might be to provide a better understanding of a unit's or regiment's history, to enable the participants to learn from past experiences by being on the ground, or to develop knowledge of command and control skills. In reality, the objectives behind such battlefield tours are as numerous as the destinations they could encompass.

It could be for any of these reasons that on 30 July 1925, a large group of officers, NCOs and cadets from the Territorial Cadet Force sailed from Dover on the cross-Channel ferry *Pieter de Conincke* bound for Ostend, their destination the scene of one of the Royal Navy's greatest engagements, Zeebrugge.

The present-day battlefield tourists, in organised commercial groups, or personal small parties, visit the places where their great-grand fathers or other distant relatives fought and fell, just as those visitors of a century ago once did. So too, do those who, like the guests of Thomas Cook, tour the ground where a generation they had never known, bled out its lifeblood.

Such was the case with four modern-day professional footballers who went in search of their predecessors in a field outside the village of Guillemont, some eight miles to the east of Albert in the region of the Somme, on an overcast morning in October 2010. The four were ex-Arsenal player and then Reading FC manager Brian McDermott, Reading's all-time top scorer Trevor Senior, former player and ex-

REMEMBERING THE FALLEN 81

REMEMBERING THE FALLEN 1914-1918 THE BATTLEFIELD TOURISTS

○ The kind of scene that many of the early battlefield visitors would have witnessed – in this case work on rebuilding Ypres underway. The sign states: 'Notice. This is Holy Ground. No stone of this fabric may be taken away. It is a heritage for all civilized peoples. By order Town Major, Ypres.'

manager Mick Gooding, and ex-captain and Welsh International Ady Williams.

The four had travelled to the Somme to discover more about Allen Foster – a swashbuckling goal scorer for Reading prior to 1914 – for a documentary about Reading FC's First World War footballing heroes. Foster had fought on the Somme with the 17th (Footballers') Battalion of the Middlesex Regiment.

By any standards Reading Football Club's contribution to the nation's war effort during the First World War was remarkable. More than forty first and reserve team players joined the Colours between 1914 and 1918. Nine did not come back; Allen Foster was one of them.

Foster, the son of a Yorkshire miner, had already passed into Reading folklore by 1914. Short, at 5'9", but stocky and entirely committed to Reading's cause, the striker had scored the winning goal against the mighty First Division Aston Villa in Reading's famous FA Cup run of 1912.

In January 1915 the 29-year-old from Kent Road near Reading's ground at Elm Park, joined the 'Footballer's Battalion' and was serving in the trenches by the end of the year along with other Reading FC players.

○ Examples of the various commercially produced souvenirs that fed a demand from visitors for mementoes of their visit.

On the Somme in 1916, the 17th Middlesex were ordered to attack ZZ Trench north of Guillemont, not much more than a stone's throw from Delville Wood and opposite the ruins of Waterlot Farm, which was an old sugar beet factory. When the whistles blew at dawn on 8 August 1916, Foster was amongst those who charged for the German line but enemy machine-gun fire caught the Footballers' Battalion in a scything crossfire. Many were killed and wounded. Foster was hit several times and went down. The attack failed.

Still alive – just – when the stretcher bearers got to him, Foster was taken back seventeen miles to a Casualty Clearing Station near the town of Corbie, east of Amiens. Unlike fellow team mates Frank Lindley and Arthur Charlton, he did not make it. When the news of his death reached Reading, the local paper declared it 'came like a thunderclap'.

Ninety-four years after the event, striker Trevor Senior – visibly moved – knelt at Allen Foster's headstone and laid a wreath in Reading's colours to honour a 'team mate' of the past. 'From one striker to an even better one', he wrote on the card.

Because of experiences such as this, there is no sign of battlefield tourism losing any of its absorbing appeal, with specialist companies having become an established part of today's blossoming tourist industry. Which means that the exploits of those courageous young men and women of the Great War will never be forgotten. ●

NOTES
1. Thorpe, Adam, 'After The War Was Over', *The Daily Telegraph*, 2 June 2001.
2. Roden, Mike, quoted on: www.aftermathww1.com
3. The full story of Lieutenant Eric Duckworth's death and his parents' remarkable pilgrimage is told by Martin Purdy and Ian Dawson in *The Gallipoli Oak* (Moonraker Publishing, 2013).

○ This view of the battlefield around Langemarck, littered by guns and wire entanglement, is typical of that which visitors to the former Western Front would have seen in the years between the wars.

82 REMEMBERING THE FALLEN

AVIATION SPECIALS

ESSENTIAL READING FROM KEY PUBLISHING

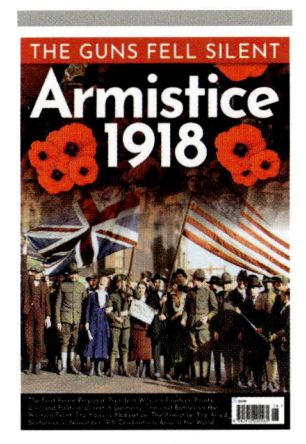

ARMISTICE 1918
This 116-page special features a graphic account of what really happened on the Western Front 100 years ago in the last few months of 1918.
£6.99 inc FREE P&P*

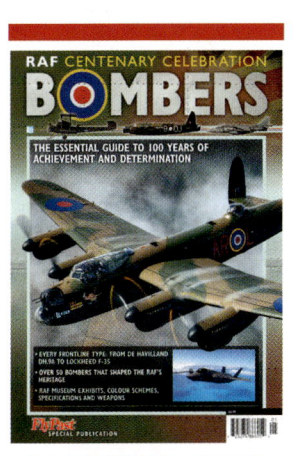

BOMBERS OF THE RAF CENTENARY
A unique 100-page tribute to the bombers that have defended Britain.
£5.99 inc FREE P&P*

1918: AN ILLUSTRATED HISTORY
This is the story of the Great War's final year.
£6.99 inc FREE P&P*

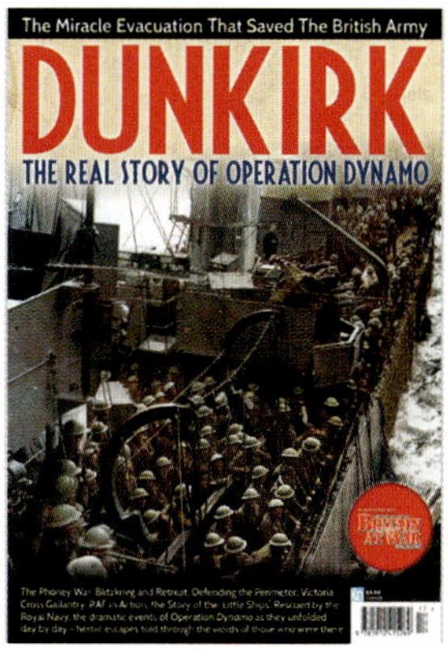

DUNKIRK
The story of the great evacuation is told, day-by-day.
£6.99 inc FREE P&P*

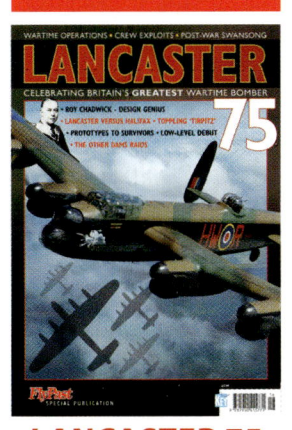

LANCASTER 75
Pays tribute to all who built, maintained and flew Lancasters, past and present.
£5.99 inc FREE P&P*

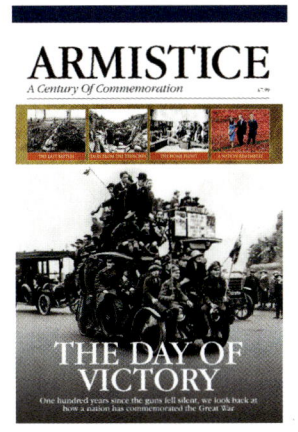

ARMISTICE
This 156-page photographic tribute looks at the war from the outbreak to that fateful day in November when the guns fell silent.
£7.99 inc FREE P&P*

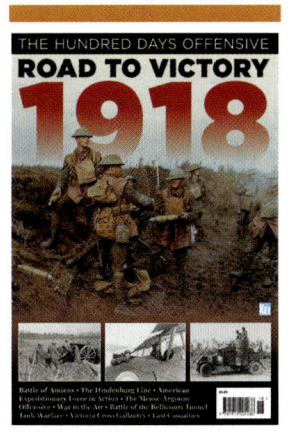

ROAD TO VICTORY
This 116-page special reveals how, after so many years of trench warfare, the fighting on the Western Front became mobile and more fluid.
£6.99 inc FREE P&P*

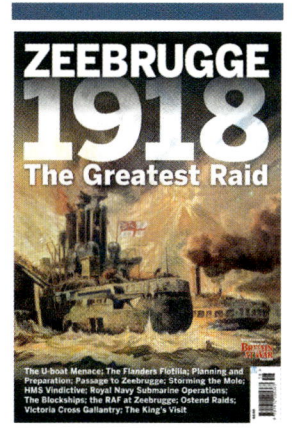

ZEEBRUGGE 1918
Key Publishing presents this special publication which commemorates the Zeebrugge raid.
£6.99 inc FREE P&P*

AVIATION SPECIALS
ESSENTIAL reading from the teams behind your FAVOURITE magazines

HOW TO ORDER

VISIT www.keypublishing.com/shop

OR

PHONE
UK: 01780 480404
ROW: (+44)1780 480404

*Prices correct at time of going to press. Free 2nd class P&P on all UK & BFPO orders. Overseas charges apply. Postage charges vary depending on total order value.

FREE Aviation Specials App 
Simply download to purchase digital versions of your favourite aviation specials in one handy place! Once you have the app, you will be able to download new, out of print or archive specials for less than the cover price!

IN APP ISSUES £3.99

902/18

REMEMBERING THE FALLEN 1914-1918 THE GREAT PILGRIMAGE

THE GREAT PILGRIMAGE

The First World War had been a conflict of epic proportions, and when the British Legion conceived of a mass pilgrimage of veterans to the battlefields of the Western Front, it was on an equally vast scale.

It was at the meeting of the National Executive Council of the British Legion in December 1926, that the idea of organising a pilgrimage to the scenes of the great battles in France and Flanders was raised. No one knew at that stage just what the response would be from the Legion's members, but the cost was fixed at £5, which, it was hoped would be a sum that would not be prohibitive. This price would include transport from London to Ostend, a two-day tour by coach or charabanc to the battlefields, with the return to London on the fourth day.

This first British Legion pilgrimage took place in the summer of 1927, but the number of veterans or family members joining the tour was disappointing. Five pounds was a lot of money for most people, and only 150 members made the trip.

Plans for a second pilgrimage for 1928 were in hand when the French authorities requested that the British Legion organise a group visit along the lines of that undertaken by the American Legion in 1927, when some 20,000 veterans and their families had sailed across the Atlantic to mark the tenth anniversary of the USA's entry into the war.

The French wanted 10,000 British ex-servicemen from across the UK to visit the battlefields in the summer of 1928 – and for them to march through the Menin Gate as Earl Haig took the salute. The former commander of the British Expeditionary Force willingly offered his support – and from that moment onwards its success was assured. By June, all 10,000 places had been filled, with demand being so great that another 1,000 men and women were added to the total.

This time, the tour would be by train, with each, loaded with 500 pilgrims,

◐ Followed by a large body of pilgrims, the Prince of Wales 'leads the standards of the Legion through Ypres' on 8 August 1928. This was the point in the Great Pilgrimage 'when all parties assembled for a service of commemoration and homage at the Menin Gate' – described as 'the grand climax to a great pilgrimage'. (All images Historic Military Press)

THE GREAT PILGRIMAGE REMEMBERING THE FALLEN 1914-1918

Major Brunel Cohen, surrounded by members of the Brussels Delegation, about to speak at the Tomb of the Unknown Warrior in Brussels, 4 August 1928. Cohen, who was badly wounded in the Third Battle of Ypres in 1917 and had both of his legs amputated, was a leading figure in the British Legion, serving as its honorary treasurer from 1921 to 1930, then as vice-chairman from 1930 to 1932, and again as honorary treasurer until 1946.

Pilgrims leaving Dover on Empress of Calais, *en route to Calais, 4 August.*

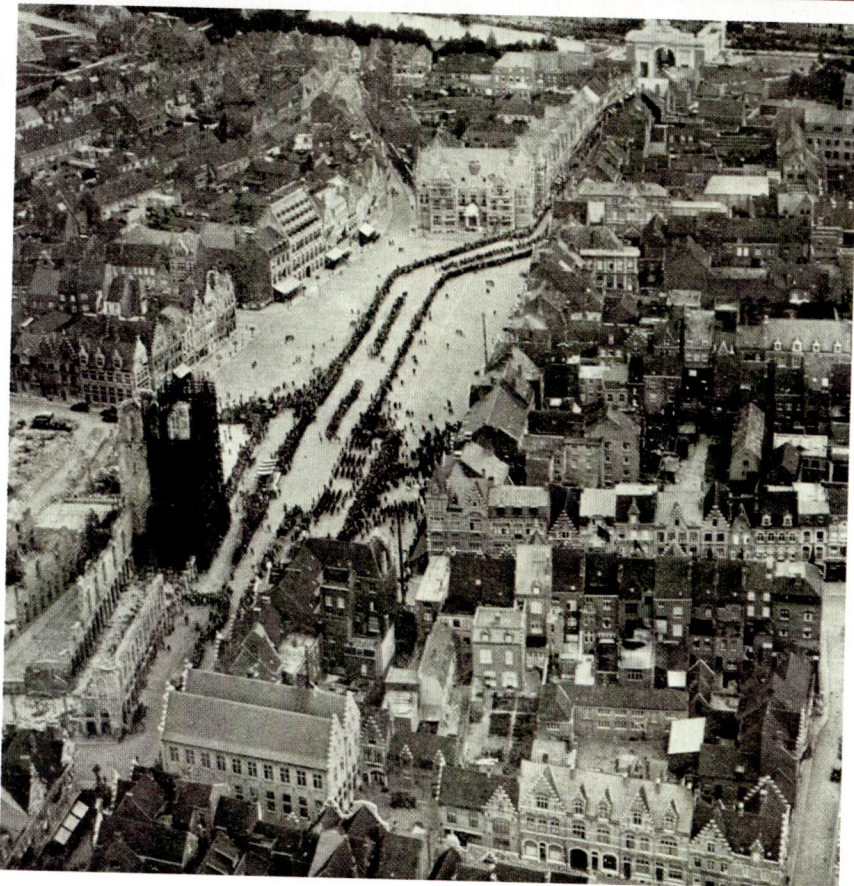

An aerial view of the British Legion's members parading through the centre of Ypres on 8 August. The reconstruction of the Cloth Hall can be seen underway at the bottom left.

starting out from each Legion Area. When the veterans reached the Continent, other trains would be waiting to take the same groups onwards to the battlefields. The train parties were divided into Companies, which varied in size with each party. Some parties formed Companies of the areas from which the pilgrims came, others formed Companies of single men, single women, and married couples.

THE OUTLINE PLAN

The pilgrims were to cross from the English ports in ten ferry boats on Saturday and Sunday the 4th and 5th of August. They would spend three nights in towns where they were to be accommodated. As the pilgrims would receive preferential treatment, in terms of both prices and 'entertainments', it was considered necessary that they should be easily identifiable. This was achieved with the issuing of Pilgrims' Badges.

The problem of what the pilgrims were to visit was a difficult one, as they were limited to those places which could be easily reached from the main railway stations, as the daily tours were to be conducted in 'cruising trains'. A preliminary reconnaissance found that the most interesting places to visit were Vimy and Beaucourt. These places would be visited on the 6th and 7th with half the pilgrims going to each. On 8 August, the whole would reunite at Ypres for a Service of Commemoration and Homage at the Menin Gate.

The planning began early in 1928, with an approach to the organisations which would have the job of getting the pilgrims to the Channel ports and across to France – the railway companies. The Southern Railway was persuaded to carry 7,500 people in twenty-four hours. In addition to its ordinary services, this meant that seven special ferry boats had to be run during the twenty-four-hour period commencing Saturday, 4 August. This left nearly one-third of the pilgrims to be carried by the other rail companies. Eventually it was arranged that the London, Midland & Scottish Railway, in conjunction with the Alsace-Lorraine Association Steamship Co., should carry 2,300 passengers by the Tilbury-Dunkirk route, and the London & North Eastern Railway Co., would take 950 on the Harwich-Zeebrugge route. The remaining pilgrims had to travel on the normal train and ferry services. The officials of these companies agreed to allow a reduction in the normal fares to enable ordinary people to afford the trip. As it transpired, despite this huge logistical undertaking, no train was more than two minutes late arriving at its destination. Medical support for the pilgrimage was to be provided by the British Red Cross.

VIMY RIDGE

The Great Pilgrimage, as it came to be known, really began with ceremonies in Paris, the chief of which was the re-kindling of the flame on the Tomb of the French Unknown Soldier by the Chairman of the British Legion, Colonel Crossfield. This ceremony was attended by a special representation from the Legion which also attended a reception hosted by the French President. A similar ceremony was held in Brussels on 4 August, with the placing of a wreath on the Tomb of the Unknown Soldier in Brussels.

The pilgrimage then began in earnest, the veterans and families visiting the battlefields. This included Vimy Ridge, which was visited by all the pilgrims. Vimy Ridge holds a unique place in the history of the First World War, in that it was the only major position on the British Front that was captured and then held throughout the rest of the war. For this reason, it was hallowed ground to those British and Canadian troops who won it and held it to the end.

The pilgrims' visit to Vimy was described by Major A. Waller: 'On the 6th, 3,500 Pilgrims arrived by train at Vimy Station, in seven trains, arriving at about ten-minute intervals. As the parties arrived from the train each was handed a packet of lunch, and the guides, who were War Graves gardeners, joined them. Those who were going up to the Ridge by bus (about 20 per cent) were directed to buses already

REMEMBERING THE FALLEN 85

REMEMBERING THE FALLEN 1914-1918 THE GREAT PILGRIMAGE

The Great Pilgrimage underway in August 1928. The original caption states that this image depicts 'the Ancre Cemetery, showing Thiepval Ridge in the background'. It adds: 'This grim, bare upland, frowning down on the British line, which, wreathed in smoke, belching with flame, and covered with their dead, was the last thing on earth many a son of old England ever saw. It still bears the scars of the trenches, and Thiepval Wood can be seen struggling to re-assert itself on the distant hill tops, to the left of where Ulster's tall granite tower tops the ridge.'

labelled with their Party letter. Others, who were going on a special visit to cemeteries, were also separated. The remainder started to walk, and by the time the last train was in, the route up to the ridge presented an impressive spectacle …

'The Mayor of Vimy and his village band greeted each train as it came in and the band played *God Save the King* continuously. This fact delayed things a little, for good Pilgrims stood to attention for some time, but finally realised that the tune was a continuous performance, and hastened to get their lunch cartons …

'The walking Pilgrims came up through Petit Vimy and Folie Wood to the [unfinished, being unveiled on 26 July 1936] Canadian Memorial. This took them just a little over an hour … After seeing the Memorial, the Pilgrims went along the Ridge Road, either walking or by the buses which left the Memorial at ten-minute intervals, to Grange Trench.

'A signal was sent off every hour to remind Pilgrims of the passing of time, and at about 2 p.m. the descent to the station started; some going by bus from Grange Trench and others walking through Folie Wood. On the way many went out of their way to see the picturesque cemetery at Petit Vimy. Arrived at the station, the different parties had their tea in the station yard; a party followed to tea as the previous party entrained.'

THIEPVAL

After Vimy, the British Legion's pilgrims jolted and rattled along the railway from Arras southwards and then northwards from Amiens until they came to the wayside station of Beaucourt-sur-Ancre. There they detrained – fathers, mothers, brothers, old and young – and in a few minutes they had wandered off in little groups.

Major Younger of the Royal Artillery wrote of their arrival: 'A grinding of brakes, a stir among the railway officials and the British Legion detrainment staff; and the train drew up at Beaucourt Station carrying the first 500 train party. At intervals of 10 to 15 minutes the procession of trains continued for the next two hours.'

The pilgrims' visit to Beaucourt was recorded in the *Daily Mail*: 'Many a Pilgrim noticed high up on a hill overlooking the valley of the Ancre, a tall granite tower with a Union Jack flapping idly atop, and doubtless wondered what memorial it was. Some of the women climbed the long slope, toiling bravely in the blazing sunshine, and ate their picnic lunches in the shadow of

The original caption states that this image depicts a small party of pilgrim's examining 'a treasure trove of war relics in Newfoundland Park'.

the tower. Very few knew over what terrible ground they had passed, and fewer still understood just where it was they were so contentedly munching ham sandwich and tomatoes.

'The hillside up which these mothers walked was Thiepval Ridge, and they ate their lunches and took off their boots to ease their aching feet on the site of the Schwaben Redoubt, in the shadow of the Memorial to the 36th (Ulster) Division …

'This grim, bare, upland, frowning down on the old British line, is sinister still today, and so it will ever be; the very air seems heavy and the light uncertain, on Thiepval Ridge twelve years after the flower of Kitchener's Army perished on its slopes.'

The pilgrims visited Y Ravine, Beaumont Hamel, Pozières, Mouquet Farm and the Newfoundland Park. At this last stop, the old trenches and dug-outs had been preserved, and barbed-wire, shells, rifles and abandoned equipment and weapons laid all around.

The pilgrims were accommodated, and warmly welcomed, by the French. The attitude of one of the locals at Lille epitomises the feelings of the French, and the lasting impression which the pilgrims had upon them: 'I did not know the British nor did I pretend to understand

The Prince of Wales, Patron of the British Legion, observing the march past in the centre of Ypres on 8 August 1928.

86 REMEMBERING THE FALLEN

THE GREAT PILGRIMAGE REMEMBERING THE FALLEN 1914-1918

Some of the pilgrims' 'climbing Vimy Ridge' on 6 August.

them. Now that they have gone, I can say thankfully that the Legion Pilgrimage has been, and will remain, one of the outstanding happenings of my whole life.'

MENIN GATE

The culminating act of remembrance for the pilgrims was the service at the Menin Gate. Again, the trains steamed in on time, to assemble for the March Past. Earl Haig, though, had recently died, and it was the Prince of Wales who took the salute, with Lady Haig bravely marching at the head of the Scottish Women's Section, in an emotional end to the great pilgrimage. 'Can anyone who was present at the final scenes at Ypres ever forget the sight of that great assemblage at the Menin Gate, with the Legion's standards lowered in honour of our dead?' asked Admiral of the Fleet, Earl Jellicoe. 'Will they not recall too, in years to come, the fine bearing of the Legionnaires, women and men, as they marched past their Royal Patron, he who has ever given his best in their service.'

From Ypres, it was the journey back to the Channel ports. 'Then home again,' wrote T.F. Lister, the First Chairman of the British Legion. 'Home! To recount the experiences of some wonderful days; home! To be prouder than ever.'

The massed ranks of the British Legion members congregating at the Menin Gate at the end of their parade through Ypres.

The Pilgrim's Badge for Party T, the members of which came from Yorkshire. This group's primary destination was Poperinghe and Ypres. The two sections of this party sailed from Harwich on 5 August.

Members of Party R or Party Q, both of which contained members of the North-West Section, 'inspecting trenches on Vimy Ridge'. They had sailed from Tilbury on 5 August.

REMEMBERING THE FALLEN 87

REMEMBERING THE FALLEN 1914-1918 THE FIELD OF REMEMBRANCE

THE FIELD OF REMEMBRANCE

Every year since 1928, in the lead-up to Remembrance Day, a Field of Remembrance is opened in the grounds of Westminster Abbey.

Like so many of the now well-established acts of commemoration, the Field of Remembrance was inspired by the actions of one individual, Major George Howson MC.

It was Major Howson who was responsible for opening the Poppy Factory in 1922. Determined to help wounded and disabled ex-servicemen, Howson had persuaded Earl Haig that the Disabled Society should supply the poppies sold in the UK – as we have seen, the first Poppy Appeal in 1921 used artificial poppies made by women and children in devastated areas of France. Haig agreed to Howson's suggestion and, with the assistance of a grant of £2,000, the latter opened a small factory off the Old Kent Road. At the time it was staffed by five ex-servicemen and was where the first 'British' poppies were manufactured.

◉ An early view of the Field of Remembrance in the grounds of St Margaret's Church, Westminster. (Historic Military Press)

◉ A recent view of the Field of Remembrance. (Brian Minkoff/Shutterstock)

88 REMEMBERING THE FALLEN

THE FIELD OF REMEMBRANCE REMEMBERING THE FALLEN 1914-1918

Miss F.M.S. Cavell, one of Nurse Edith Cavell's two sisters, plants a memorial cross in the nurses' plot of what was then known as the Empire Field of Remembrance, 7 November 1937.

Within ten years, the name had changed to The Poppy Factory and Howson was employing over 350 disabled veterans to make the poppies. The factory moved to Richmond in 1925. Three years later, Howson and a small group of disabled veterans gathered around a simple wooden cross in the grounds of St Margaret's Church in Westminster. Armed with a tray of poppies and a collecting tin, they invited passers-by to plant a poppy beside the cross. Though only a handful of poppies were planted, the first Field of Remembrance was born.

On 1 August 1932, a new element to the Field of Remembrance was enacted at the *Thiepval Anglo-French Cemetery*. The cemetery is located beside the Thiepval Memorial, which was, as will be explained later in more detail, unveiled on the same day. The *Edinburgh Evening News* of 29 July gave the following description: 'One minute's silence will be observed, and the [Thiepval Memorial's unveiling] ceremony will conclude with the French and British National Anthems, after the sounding of the *Reveille*. Permission has been granted for ashes of crosses planted in the British Legion field of remembrance at Westminster Abbey to be scattered in the Anglo-French cemetery adjoining the memorial, and arrangements have been made for this duty to be undertaken during the unveiling ceremony by one of the disabled ex-Service men who made these crosses.'

The ashes, which were referred to as the 'Ashes of Remembrance' in some quarters, were all that was remained of the crosses from the previous year's Field of Remembrance, the crosses themselves having been 'recently cremated at the British Legion Poppy Factory at Richmond'.

The following year the ceremony was repeated, but this time at *Faubourg d'Amiens Cemetery* in Arras on 6 August 1933. In a special 'declaration of war ceremony', led on this occasion by Major-General Sir Fabian Ware, ashes were scattered across the cemetery. It is worth noting that in 1933 it was reported in the papers that poppies were being planted in the Field of Remembrance at an average rate of 200 per hour.

On 4 August 1935, the ceremony was enacted at *Vlamertinghe Military Cemetery* a couple of miles west of Ypres town centre. Veterans attending the former Western Front to mark the anniversary of the outbreak of war were once again invited to participate in scattering across the cemetery.

As the scattering ceremony continued to grow in scale, by 1939 individual British Legion branches that had their own fields of remembrance were also sending their crosses to Richmond to be cremated. That year the ashes were scattered at Cabaret-Rouge British Cemetery on 7 August. Situated between two war cemeteries, one French and the other German, Cabaret-Rouge British Cemetery lies south of the town of Souchez in France. The cemetery contains more than 7,650 burials of servicemen of the British Empire in the First World War. The name Cabaret Rouge was taken from a small café, a brick building with red tiles that was distinctive in the village where most of the houses were thatched. It stood less than a mile south of Souchez and was destroyed by heavy shelling in May 1915.

Still organised by The Poppy Factory, the Field of Remembrance has developed over the years into an impressive undertaking that encompasses 350 plots for regimental and other associations that are laid out in the area between Westminster Abbey and St. Margaret's Church. Remembrance crosses are still provided so that ex-service men and women, as well as members of the public, can plant a cross in memory of their fallen comrades and loved ones. The Field is opened every Thursday before Remembrance Sunday and stays open for a further ten days.

A visitor to the Field of Remembrance plants a cross in one of the many plots. (Brian Minkoff/Shutterstock)

REMEMBERING THE FALLEN 89

REMEMBERING THE FALLEN 1914-1918 A GREAT WAR 'BAYEUX TAPESTRY'

A GREAT WAR 'BAYEUX TAPESTRY'

It is almost impossible to list the diversity in style and form that the many memorials which came in to being after the First World War have taken. Without doubt among the more unusual is the North Staffordshire Territorial Force's panoramic memorial canvas.

In 2010, while searching for stories connected with the First World War Army camps constructed across Cannock Chase in Staffordshire, two members of a local military research group, The Chase Project, came across an interesting article. From this the two researchers learnt that three days before the Armistice was signed in November 1918 there had been an appeal for information to help compile a history of two Territorial Force battalions of the North Staffordshire Regiment (Prince of Wales's), the 1/5th and 1/6th, during the First World War. The majority of the men and officers of the two battalions were from Stoke, Hanley, Newcastle, Stone, Stafford, Leeke, Uttoxeter and surrounding villages.

Other than being of passing interest, this was largely forgotten by the pair until they stumbled upon a comment from 1929 about a desire to mark the tenth annual reunion of the 5th North Staffs in a special way. It was decided at the time that this commemoration would take the form of a 'memorial canvas' which would detail the part the two battalions played in the Great War.

With the impending centenary of the beginning of the First World War fast approaching, the two men in question, Richard Pursehouse and Lee Dent, considered the idea of creating a replica of that memorial canvas if, indeed, it still existed. They began their quest to find it by contacting the Staffordshire Regiment Museum at Whittington near Lichfield. The staff there stated they had no records, although military author and museum researcher Jeffrey Elson did know of the canvas, but not of its whereabouts.

However, in due course the museum reported that it had been offered the canvas by the Potteries' Museum, which had, at some time, acquired it. Unfortunately, the Staffordshire Regiment Museum had neither the space to display it or to store it under the right conditions. Such issues aside, the canvas had been rediscovered!

THE TERRITORIALS

After training at Luton in Bedfordshire, the 1/5th North Staffs, which was part of the North Midland Division, arrived in France in March 1915. The division, which changed its name to change to the 46th (North Midland) Division on 12 May 1915, was rightly proud of the fact that it was the first full Territorial Division to land on French soil.

For the next three years the 1/5th fought alongside the 1/6th North Staffs, as well as their sister Territorial battalions of the 1/5th South Staffs and 1/6th South Staffs as part of the 137th (Staffordshire) Brigade. Then, on 29 January 1918, with the recent contraction

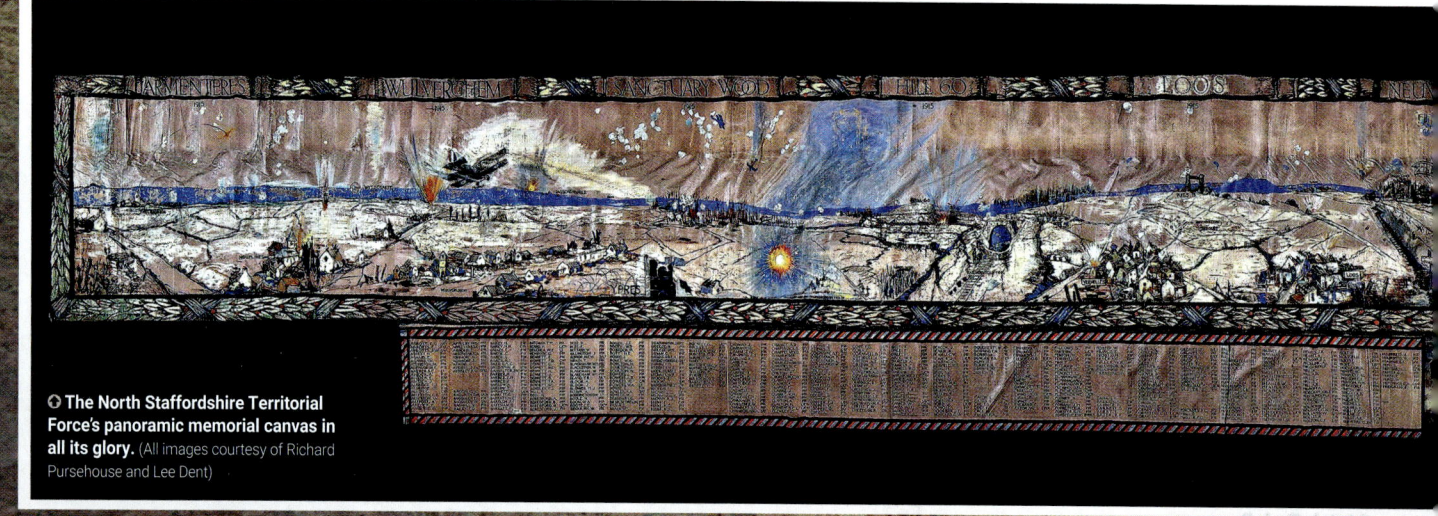

○ The North Staffordshire Territorial Force's panoramic memorial canvas in all its glory. (All images courtesy of Richard Pursehouse and Lee Dent)

A GREAT WAR 'BAYEUX TAPESTRY' REMEMBERING THE FALLEN 1914-1918

from four to three battalions per brigade in the British Army, the 1/5th North Staffs was disbanded, and most of the men transferred to various South and North Staffs battalions, with some joining the newly-created 5th (as opposed to 1/5th, 2/5th 3/5th etc) Battalion North Staffs the day after.

The men of the 137th (Staffordshire) Brigade fought in several major battles, at Neuve Chapelle, Loos (including the infamous Hohenzollern Redoubt), the diversionary attack at Gommecourt on the Somme on 1 July 1916, and, in 1918, the breaching of the Hindenburg Line.

While it was the case that although the main focus of the memorial canvas was on the 1/5th North Staffs, as the four Territorial Force battalions of the South and North Staffs fought alongside each other for virtually the whole war the canvas was effectively a representation of all four battalions. Such was the *esprit de corps* between them, it is an epitaph to all of their Great War exploits.

⊙ One of the North Staffs' reunion dinners held at Hanley.

⊙ Some of the artists at work on the canvas in 1929.

Once back in North Staffordshire, life settled into a semblance of normality for the battle-hardened veterans. In a desire to raise a glass to remember 'absent comrades', a simple reunion evening was organised by the 5th Battalion of the North Staffordshire Regiment (as they became known from 1920, dropping the 'Prince of Wales'). The date was 10 June 1920, and the venue was King's Hall in Stoke-on-Trent. The event was organised for those who had served with any battalions of the North Staffordshire Regiment during the Great War.

The occasion was a resounding success, so much so that it was agreed the event should be repeated and that the date moved to the beginning of the year. The response from those present meant the subsequent reunions expanded in size during the following nine years, each therefore increasing in its complexity. ➡

REMEMBERING THE FALLEN **91**

REMEMBERING THE FALLEN 1914-1918 A GREAT WAR 'BAYEUX TAPESTRY'

Some of the artists at work on the canvas in 1929.

Richard Pursehouse with the Memorial Canvas during a recent unveiling.

A MEMORIAL CANVAS

Eventually the question arose among the veterans as to how to mark the tenth reunion meal in February 1929, with discussions often centring on the possibility of a way of representing the history of the battalion during the Great War. It was at this point that Major Tom Simpson and Mr N.H. Slater came up with the concept of a memorial canvas. The idea was presented to Mr G. Forsyth, the Art Director for the City of Stoke-on-Trent, after which it was accepted by the organisation as a whole.

The original plan was to create the memorial canvas as a series of panoramic battle scenes to fill the entire wall of the Grand Hotel in Hanley, where the reunion meal was to take place. In fact, the canvas was constructed in eleven sections, or 'episodes', which were approximately 6 feet wide. The total length was some 69 feet.

The size of the canvas necessary for the project resulted in the Art Director selecting the School of Art at Burslem as the venue for the task. Two of the artists involved in creating the panels, Mr W. Sheard and Mr Cyril Johnson, were both former members of the battalion, as was Mr Gordon Dyke who supplied the actual base canvas material. Interestingly, in 1915 Sheard had sketched a drawing entitled *Potters Forever!* which depicted the 1/5th Battalion attacking at Loos for publication in *The Sentinel*, a local newspaper. He had also sent home drawings of life in the trenches.

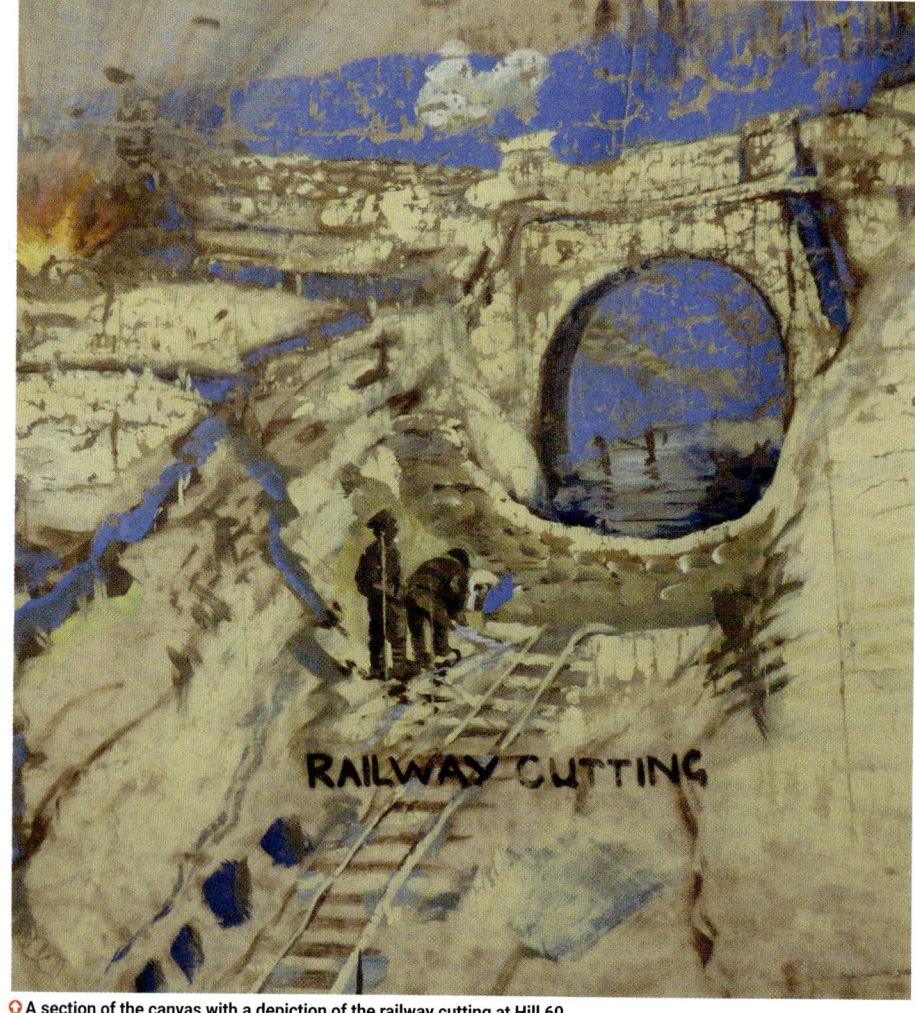

A section of the canvas with a depiction of the railway cutting at Hill 60.

The regimental badge as depicted on the Memorial.

Other artists who participated in the project and who had also taken part in some of the fighting added aspects of the events that they remembered, such as distant artillery fire, bursting shrapnel, falling scout balloons, aerial battles and troops advancing. The team of artists was headed by Miss M. Davenport, who was aided by Mr H. Landon, Mr J. Bromley, Mr H. Plant, Miss Cartlidge, Miss H Lloyd, and Miss Florence Elsby. The scenes were edged with a scroll of the regimental colours of silver, red, and black.

The project began in mid-December 1928 and took fourteen days to complete. The oil paints were supplied by Walpamur Co. Ltd., originally The Wallpaper Company, which today is the Arthur Sanderson Company. The scenes were painted in a monochrome style, with a single continuous blue line of the distant landscape binding the whole design. The vivid blue pantone selected for the latter was a nod to Wedgwood Blue,

92 REMEMBERING THE FALLEN

A GREAT WAR 'BAYEUX TAPESTRY' REMEMBERING THE FALLEN 1914-1918

BALCOMBE'S GREAT WAR MURAL

The village of Balcombe in West Sussex possess what is quite possibly a unique memorial – a series of dramatic 'war and peace' frescos that adorn the walls of the community's Victory Hall.

Built around an existing community centre, the building itself was completed in 1923 to remember all the men of the village who served in the First World War; their names, over 200 in total, are inscribed on a wooden panel inside the main entrance. The hall was funded by both public subscription and the generosity of Lady Denham who lived in Balcombe Place. It was Lord Denham who led the unveiling on 10 November 1923. Three days later the *Mid Sussex Times* reported on Balcombe's achievements:

'In many parts of the country similar halls with the same object in view as theirs had been built, and no doubt in many cases in towns and cities, larger and more spacious than their own. But they could fairly claim for theirs the added note of distinction the frescoes which adorned the walls, the work of that well-known artist, Major Lytton. Major Lytton himself did good service the war, and with his experience as a soldier and the trained eye of the artist he had depicted a scene of frequent occurrence: a relief party going up to the front line while action was in progress. On the left they saw German prisoners, in the centre stretcher bearers and on the right men of the relief party, and in the background the stricken tree trunks and buildings shattered shell fire.'

It was Lady Denham who had commissioned Neville Lytton, a close friend of hers, to complete the frescos. He did so by applying the paint to wet lime plaster, and, as the paint dried on the plaster, his painting became in effect part of the building. Lytton, having served in the Royal Sussex Regiment and completed postings as a war correspondent, was already a respected war artist – in the immediate aftermath of the First World War both the Imperial War Museum and Musée de Guerre acquired examples of his work.

In 1920 Lytton wrote the book *The Press and the General Staff* outlining the grim realities of his experiences. The very last sentence of it reads: 'I came to the conclusion that no one but a madman could ever wish for war; the highly polished boots, the bright buttons, the glittering medals and the clicking of spurred heels must never again deceive humanity into thinking that war is anything but the blackest tragedy from start to finish.' (Images by Robert Mitchell, with the kind permission of the Victory Hall Management Committee)

REMEMBERING THE FALLEN 93

REMEMBERING THE FALLEN 1914-1918 A GREAT WAR 'BAYEUX TAPESTRY'

○ Lee Dent examines the first section of the North Staffordshire Territorial Force's panoramic memorial canvas.

as members of the Wedgwood family had served in the Staffs.

Each panel depicts a key episode in the North Staff's Great War history. From the regiment's baptism of fire on the Western Front at Armentières in April 1915, they continue on through the fighting at Wulverghem (near Messines to the south of Ypres), to Sanctuary Wood (Ypres 1915), Hill 60 (again Ypres in 1915), the Battle of Loos, Neuve Chapelle, and Neuville St Vaast (between Arras and Vimy Ridge). The next panel depicts the bitter fighting at Gommecourt Park (a diversionary attack during the Battle of the Somme in 1916), after which comes the Ransart Sector, the Lievin Sector in 1916 (in front of the French town of Lens) and, finally, the St Quentin Canal in September 1918 and the capture of the Riqueval Bridge during the smashing of the Hindenburg Line.

THE CANVAS IS COMPLETED

With the work done, the completed canvas was unveiled at the annual reunion in February 1929, this being held at the Grand Hotel in Hanley. It was after the meal had ended that the canvas was revealed, after which a silent toast to 'Absent Comrades' was given by Colonel Blizzard.

The reunions continued all through the 1930s, with the memorial canvas taking pride of place on each occasion. It is known that there were various adjustments made to the design, including aeroplanes being added and subtracted.

On several occasions Victoria Cross holders connected to the North and South Staffordshire regiments, or who were born in the Potteries, were invited. This included Brigadier General John Vaughan Campbell *VC*, CMG, DSO, dubbed the 'Tally HO VC', who had in 1918 orchestrated the successful attack on the Hindenburg Line of German defences at its strongest point. This feat of arms has been described as the 'day the men of Staffordshire won the war' by Potteries-born historian Dr John Bourne.

In the mid-1930s an alphabetically-named Roll of Honour, listing over 900 who served with the battalion, was attached along the bottom, with a silhouetted soldier with his rifle slung over his shoulder directly below the central battalion crest.

The 5th North Staffs' reunions were well supported throughout the 1930s, with often some 300 or more attending. At the same time, other battalions held similar reunions; in February 1932, for example, the veterans of the 6th North Staffs held their reunion in Burton, and the 7th North Staffs at the Copeland Hotel in Stoke. It was during the latter that a Book of Remembrance containing over 1,000 names of those who had served in the battalion was presented to Stoke Parish Church. In 1937 the 7th North Staffs reunion (its sixteenth) took place within days of the 5th North Staffs at the Grand Hotel in Hanley.

At the 1940 reunion, the former members of the 5th North Staffs agreed to be incorporated with the 41st Anti-Aircraft Battalion (Searchlights) RE association. Then in 1945 the decision was taken to take the canvas away for conservation. In 1946 a lower-key reunion took place at the North Stafford Hotel in Hanley, where Colonel Blizzard was presented with a silver salver for organising so many of the reunions since 1919. In February 1947, after a lapse of seven years a 'full blown' reunion was held at Fenton Town Hall, attended by over 250 former 5th North Staffs men.

In 1948, the reunion was held at the Prince's Hall in Burslem. Still attended by nearly 300 individuals, once again the 'panorama of the battlefields' formed a back drop to the top table. In November 1948 the 5th North Staffs were involved in 'an impressive ceremony' at Stoke Town Hall when three stained glass windows were presented to the Lord Mayor.

Even in the 1950s the reunions were still taking place; that in 1953 was held

○ The Roll of Honour has been added below the canvas in this view of the reunion in 1947.

in the Jubilee Hall, Stoke-on-Trent, with a 'background of a large pictorial map of France, where the old regiment distinguished itself'. By this time, reunions of Second World War Staffordshire Regiment veterans were being organised and the two county regiments were amalgamating.

The canvas was stored away, only occasionally seeing the light of day. It eventually found its way to the Potteries' Museum.

It was at the Potteries' Museum on Saturday, 22 September 2018, that this remarkable canvas memorial once again went on display, allowing the current generations to see this unique and fitting epitaph to those from the North Staffordshire Regiment who fought and died in the First World War. ●

○ A scene of the St Quentin canal as it was during the fighting on 29 September 1918.

94 REMEMBERING THE FALLEN

FROM PROPELLERS TO GLOBES **REMEMBERING THE FALLEN 1914-1918**

FROM PROPELLERS TO GLOBES

The commemoration of aircrew who died during the First World War, whether in training, through an accident or in combat, has resulted in a number of unusual memorials.

It had been just eleven years before the start of the First World War that an aeroplane had taken to the skies for the first time, covering a distance of just 120 feet. In August 1914 the Royal Flying Corps amounted to just five squadrons, which between them mustered no more than fifty serviceable aircraft. In addition, the Royal Naval Air Service had started the war with ninety-three aircraft, six airships, and two balloons.

As the war progressed, the developments in aerial warfare were staggering. By the time the Armistice was agreed in 1918, the Royal Air Force, formed in April the same year through the amalgamation of the RFC and the RNAS, was not only the oldest independent air force in the world, it was also the largest. On the day that the fighting came to a halt the RAF could muster some 22,647 aircraft of all types, a number that included 3,300 on first-line strength and 103 airships.

A new form of warfare had been born, though for the air arms of the British military the cost had been high. In the course of the war, note John Ellis and Michael Cox in *The World War I Databook*, the UK had lost 35,970 aircraft, of which some 4,000 were combat losses. Including wounded, missing and those who became prisoners of war, a total of 16,620 aircrew were casualties. Of this number, 6,170 lost their lives.[1]

◯ Allied graves in a cemetery near Hesdin, France, on 14 July 1918. A number the burials are those of RAF airmen, their graves being marked by sections of propellers acting as temporary headstones. After the war such markers would be replaced by standard Imperial War Graves Commission headstones. (NARA)

REMEMBERING THE FALLEN **95**

REMEMBERING THE FALLEN 1914-1918 FROM PROPELLERS TO GLOBES

It quickly became an established practice to mark the graves of aircrew with parts of an aircraft, often sections of a propeller. One father, who had just visited his son's grave in a cemetery near Doullens, was quoted during a debate in the House of Commons on 17 December 1919: 'Some of these have crosses made out of aeroplane propellers, parts of aeroplanes, and in the case of my son a cross of iron made out of a smashed motor lorry and an aeroplane with the centre made in brass from a shell case fired on the field, there exists a permanent memorial. It was made by his brother officers as a personal tribute.'

On a number of occasions these grave markers were erected by the enemy. During an advance in December 1917, across territory previously held by the Germans, Second Lieutenant Huntley Gordon recalled coming across the grave of 24-year-old Lieutenant John George Will. In a letter he sent home Gordon noted the following:

○ The temporary grave marker made from the propeller of the aircraft flown by Second Lieutenant Kenneth Turner Campbell, 210 Squadron RAF, who was killed in action on 17 June 1918. He was buried in Pernes British Cemetery. (Department of National Defence/Library and Archives Canada)

○ An Indian Sepoy at the grave of two British airmen who were shot down during the Mesopotamian Campaign. Their grave is marked by the propeller from their aircraft. (NARA)

'Round the propeller-hub is painted "2nd Lt J.G. Will RFC". He was the wing-three quarter known before the war as "the flying Scot" ... The grave must have been made by Boche airmen – a curiously chivalrous act, for they can hardly have thought it likely that we would advance far enough to see it.'[2]

A former Scotland international rugby football player, Will had volunteered to transfer from the Leinster Regiment to the Royal Flying Corps in November 1915. He gained his Wings in June the following year.

Early in the morning of 25 March 1917, Will took off from Le Hameau at the controls of a 29 Squadron Nieuport 17 Scout (that with the serial number A6751). He was one of a number of pilots detailed to provide fighter escort to a FE.2b undertaking a dawn photographic reconnaissance patrol.

However, two of the FE.2b's escort never returned. Passing over the German front line, the RFC pilots encountered formidable opposition in the form of Jagdgeschwader 1, the infamous 'Flying Circus' led by Manfred Albrecht Freiherr von Richthofen, the Red Baron. In the ensuing dogfight it would appear that Will was shot down by Lothar Freiherr von Richthofen, the Red Baron's younger brother, whilst Lieutenant Christopher Guy Gilbert fell to the guns of the Red Baron himself

Gilbert's Nieuport came down near the village of Tilloy-lès-Mofflaines, to the south-east of Arras. He was pulled from the burning wreckage of his aircraft by German soldiers and taken prisoner still wearing his pyjamas – he had decided *not* to dress before taking-off and just pulled on a flying jacket over his bed clothes! Gilbert survived the experience of being the Red Baron's 31st victory, albeit badly injured.

In the years after the war many of the early improvised grave markers, along with the wooden crosses that more often than not surrounded them, were replaced with standard IWGC headstones. It is the surviving memorials, erected in the

○ The obelisk and globe that form the basis of the Arras Flying Services Memorial can be seen on the right of this view of part of the Faubourg-d'Amiens Cemetery. (Pecold/Shutterstock.com)

96 REMEMBERING THE FALLEN

FROM PROPELLERS TO GLOBES **REMEMBERING THE FALLEN 1914-1918**

CAPTAIN ROBERT 'BOB' LITTLE

A portrait of Captain Robert Alexander 'Bob' Little. Little was born in Melbourne on 19 July 1895. He enlisted in the RNAS in 1915. Having trained as a pilot at Hendon at his own expense, he qualified on 27 October 1916, after which he was commissioned. On 27 May 1918, Little was flying a Camel at night in search of Gotha bombers and was attacking a machine that was caught in a searchlight beam when he was struck by a bullet from the Gotha's gunners or from the ground. It passed through both thighs, causing him to crash-land. He bled to death before help arrived. Little's total score was at least forty-seven destroyed or out of control, with others forced to land or driven down. He was the most successful Australian fighter pilot of the war. In this case the centre of the propeller of his Triplane was not used as a grave marker, but turned into a clock by Little's fellow airmen shortly after his death and was presented to his widow. (Courtesy of the Australian War Memorial; A05200)

memory of some of the aircrew casualties, that provide a more varied, if not unique, means of commemoration – as the following selection testifies.

THE ARRAS FLYING SERVICES MEMORIAL

Though it had initially been located by British troops at the end of 1917, Lieutenant John Will's grave was subsequently lost. He is, therefore, one of the nearly 1,000 men listed on the Arras Flying Services Memorial.

In the form of an obelisk surmounted by a globe, the memorial is located just inside the Faubourg-d'Amiens Cemetery, which is adjacent to the Boulevard du General de Gaulle in the western part of the town of Arras. It commemorates 985 airmen of the Royal Naval Air Service, the Royal Flying Corps, the Australian Flying Corps and the Royal Air Force, either by attachment from other arms of the forces of the Commonwealth or by original enlistment, who were killed across the Western Front and who have no known grave.

◯ One of the 985 airmen commemorated on the Arras Flying Services Memorial is Major Edward Corringham 'Mick' Mannock VC, DSO & Two Bars, MC & Bar. Among the most decorated servicemen in the British armed forces, Mannock was shot down in flames by ground fire as he crossed the German lines on 26 July 1918. His body was never found or identified. This picture of Mannock was taken at St Omer in June 1918. (Courtesy of the Mark Hillier Collection)

◯◯ This temporary wooden marker was placed on the grave of Flight Commander Robert A. Little, DSO & Bar, DSC & Bar, of 203 Squadron RAF (formerly No.3 Squadron RNAS), who was killed on 27 May 1918 (see above left). Little was initially buried in the village cemetery at Nœux, where it is assumed this picture was taken, before his body was exhumed and moved to Wavans British Cemetery. (Department of National Defence/Library and Archives Canada)

◯ A Canadian soldier examines a German airman's grave, which includes part of the propeller of his aircraft, in December 1917. (Department of National Defence/Library and Archives Canada)

REMEMBERING THE FALLEN **97**

REMEMBERING THE FALLEN 1914-1918 FROM PROPELLERS TO GLOBES

○ An unusual memorial to a Great War pilot. When 23-year-old Captain The Hon. Eric Fox Pitt Lubbock, of 43 Squadron RFC, was shot down over Belgium in 1917 his grief stricken mother, Lady Avebury, commissioned a touching memorial in the shape of his aircraft, a Sopwith Camel, to stand forever in the grounds of her family estate – which is now High Elms Country Park in the London Borough of Bromley. Lubbock, who fell to the guns of the German Ace Leutnant *Paul Strähle*, was buried in Lijssenthoek Military Cemetery, Belgium. (Courtesy of Robert Mitchell)

It was originally planned to hold the memorial's official unveiling ceremony on 15 May 1932, but it had to be postponed after the President of the French Republic, Paul Doumer, was assassinated by a Russian émigré. The inauguration finally went ahead on 31 July. The following account of the unveiling, which took place at the same time as the main Arras Memorial, was published in *The Times* the following day:

'On the four sides of this obelisk, which forms more particularly the Air Services' memorial on this spot, are those of airmen. The men who bore them came from our own countries and from all the great Dominions; they died above all parts of the Western Front, or far beyond it over Germany; they fell in the early days of the War, when squadrons were few and their duties hardly defined; in the middle period, when the mastery of the air inclined this way and that as construction and tactics evolved; in the last days, when the independent Air Force was preparing those final offensives which the armistice with Germany forestalled.

'Here, about the centre of the British Western Front, are named the representatives of all in the Royal Naval Air Service, the Royal Flying Corps, and the Royal Air Force who came to the Western Front and went home through the heights.

'The globe placed on the obelisk has a significance bridging the years that have passed since November, 1918. It stands exactly, with its north and south points, as our globe hung in space on the morning of Armistice Day, 1918. On every anniversary of that morning it will recall the sacrifice that these kinsmen of ours made, winning infinite peace for themselves in the struggle to win peace for their country, and it will catch, however faintly, the warmth of the sun that shone down that day on the trenches of the Arras Front, when at last no sound came from the distant guns and Death rode no longer on the airman's wings.'

The memorial as a whole was designed by Sir Edwin Lutyens, who was responsible for the entire layout of the Faubourg-d'Amiens Cemetery. Meanwhile, the renowned Scottish sculptor Sir William Reid Dick created the globe, which measures four-foot six inches in diameter and weighs almost three tons, as well as the badges on the monument. The latter are those of the

○ A portrait of Captain Eric Horace Comber-Taylor. (Historic Military Press)

○ Various views of Captain Eric Horace Comber-Taylor's original grave marker. It was whilst taking off from 10 Squadron's base at Droglandt aerodrome that the engine of his Bristol F2B failed. Though Comber-Taylor (pictured on the left) was killed in the ensuing crash, his observer, Second Lieutenant G.A. Cameron, was seriously injured (though some accounts state he was uninjured). Comber-Taylor was buried in Esquelbecq Military Cemetery. (Historic Military Press)

Royal Naval Air Service, the Royal Flying Corps and the Royal Air Force, as well as the combined badges of Canada, Australia, New Zealand, and South Africa.

DEFENDING BRITAIN'S SKIES

On the evening of 7 March 1918, Riesenflieger-Abteilung 501 despatched six of its so-called 'Giant' bombers to attack London, though one turned back when an engine seized. Of the remaining raiders, three reached London – though they all kept the British defences busy and that night, the anti-aircraft guns firing a total of 9,737 rounds.[3]

FROM PROPELLERS TO GLOBES REMEMBERING THE FALLEN 1914-1918

◯ Standing on Castle Hill on the moors overlooking Egton Bridge in North Yorkshire, this memorial commemorates one of the thousands of airmen who lost their lives whilst training in the UK. Francis Holt Yates Titcomb RN was a Probationary Flight Officer in the Royal Naval Air Service. On the morning of 15 April 1917, he took off from the RNAS Flying Training airfield at Redcar in a Maurice Farman Longhorn, serial N5055, to undertake what was to be his first solo cross-country flight. Unfortunately, Titcomb became disorientated in snow clouds whilst flying over the Moors; at 12.05 hours his aircraft crashed upside down on Castle Hill, which can be found between Egton Bridge and Goathland. Local people found Titcomb in the wreckage and carried him on a farm gate to nearby High Burrows Farm where he died soon after. He was 19-years-old. This memorial, known locally as the Swinsty Cross, was erected under the instruction of Mr J.K. Foster JP, of Egton Manor, in the early part of 1929. It stands close to the crash site. (Courtesy of D. Twigg; www.geograh.org.uk)

◯ A view of some of the graves in Bailleul Communal Cemetery Extension, Nord. The grave marker made from a propeller that can be seen in the centre denotes the last resting place of the RFC ace Captain Donald Charles Cunnell. Serving on 20 Squadron, Cunnell was killed by German anti-aircraft fire near Wervick, Belgium, on 12 July 1917; his observer, Lieutenant A.G. Bill, managed to fly the aircraft back to base. Just six days earlier, Cunnell, flying a FE.2d (serial A6412) with Second Lieutenant Albert Edward Woodbridge, gained fame for his part in shooting down and wounding the Red Baron. (Alexander Turnbull Library/National Library of New Zealand)

A number of aircraft from the various Home Defence squadrons were also scrambled. Among the latter was a Royal Aircraft Factory *B.E.12* (serial number C3208) flown by Captain Alexander Bruce Kynoch, who was serving in 37 Squadron, and a Royal Aircraft Factory (serial B679) with Captain Henry Clifford Stroud, of 61 Squadron, at the controls. The pair had taken-off from Stow Maries and Rochford respectively.

The darkness and less than ideal weather conditions that night (a number of sorties had been grounded for this reason) led to disaster as the two men collided over the village of Shotgate. The two aircraft fell to the ground at Dollymans Farm, crashing in adjacent fields.

Formerly of the Duke of Wellington's Regiment, Kynoch had previously served in Gallipoli, Egypt, and Macedonia. For his part, Stroud had served as a subaltern in the Royal Engineers on the Western Front from August 1914 to February 1915, at which point he was badly wounded in the legs. Following his recovery, he was posted to the Northern Bombing School at Otley in Yorkshire where he was an instructor in both Field Engineering and Bombing.

Both men were killed in the collision, and, as Historic England's records reveal, their crash sites are today being marked by a pair of memorials: '[These] were erected around 1920, marking the spot where each pilot was found by William Woodburn Wilson of nearby Great Fanton Hall in North Benfleet who, accompanied by his sister Jean, was the first to arrive at the scene of the fatal crash.

'It is believed that Mr Wilson erected a nine-foot cross at each memorial, and each of the monuments is shown as a 'Cross' on the 1922 and 1939 Ordnance Survey maps. It appears these "crosses" were formed of the propellers of the crashed planes, as Mr Wilson's sister Jean referred to them as "propeller memorials" in a letter published in *Essex Countryside* magazine in January 1960. In this letter, Ms Woodburn Wilson states: "When my brother sold the property he had it incorporated in the title deeds that these two small plots were not included in the sale, were still his property, and were to be forever held sacred."'[4]

A LUTYENS LINK

It is sadly the case that during training the risks were extremely high with the death toll amongst pilots in training in the United Kingdom being around 8,000 by the end of the First World War. Prior to 1917, when a more formalised method of training was introduced, fatalities numbered six or seven a day.[5]

Often early pilot training was carried out on very basic machines, with pilots sometimes receiving only two to three hours' dual instruction before being expected to go solo. Cecil Lewis was

◯ The memorial marking the death of 61 Squadron's Captain Henry Clifford Stroud, of 61 Squadron. (Courtesy of Terry Joyce; www.geograph.org.uk)

REMEMBERING THE FALLEN 99

REMEMBERING THE FALLEN 1914-1918 FROM PROPELLERS TO GLOBES

A short distance from the memorial to Captain Stroud is this one commemorating the other pilot killed in the same accident - Captain Alexander Bruce Kynoch. (Courtesy of Terry Joyce; www.geograph.org.uk)

The original grave of 1st Lieutenant Quentin Roosevelt, a pilot with the 95th Aero Squadron. The youngest son of President Theodore Roosevelt, he was shot down and killed on Bastille Day, 14 July 1918. Roosevelt was buried by German personnel, the grave including parts of his aircraft. After his grave came under Allied control, thousands of American soldiers visited it to pay their respects – which is when this image was taken – and new name plates were added. (NARA)

This propeller memorial, located in St. John's Church at Longside in Aberdeenshire, commemorates an entire crew, and not of an aircraft but an airship. Operating from Longside Airship Station at Lenabo, the Coastal Class airship C.25 was searching for a reported damaged U-boat when it was last heard of at 18.40 hours on 31 July 1918, some '60 miles East of Aberdeen'. The exact circumstances leading to C.25's loss are not known, though it is generally stated that it was shot down by a U-boat underway on the surface. This propeller, from C.25's aft 22hp Renault engine, was recovered floating on the water at the crash site. (Courtesy of Iain Smith; www.geograph.org.uk)

one such airmen, recalling: 'One and a half hours' dual stood to my credit. I had trundled round the aerodrome with Sergeant Yates my instructor, doing left hand circuits, and made a few indifferent landings.' At this point, Lewis' instructor was happy to allow him to go solo in the afternoon – if wind was right![6]

It was not only in training that the risk of disaster was high; it was equally so in experimental units. On 8 May 1918, Lieutenant Lionel Francis Derek Lutyens had taken off from Farnborough in Airco DH.4 A7671. Serving at the Royal Aircraft Establishment (RAE), Lutyens was an experienced aviator who had flown experimental aircraft of all types for several months. His passenger that day was a

This bronze plaque commemorating Lieutenant William Barnard Rhodes-Moorhouse VC can be found embedded in a tree just off the road through Melplash in Dorset – a short from Parnham where he is buried. Rhodes-Moorhouse was fatally injured during his VC action, as the citation reveals: 'For most conspicuous bravery on 26th April, 1915, in flying to Courtrai and dropping bombs on the railway line near that station. On starting the return journey he was mortally wounded, but succeeded in flying for 35 miles to his destination, at a very low altitude, and reported the successful accomplishment of his object. He has since died of his wounds.' (Courtesy of Nigel Mykura; www.geograph.org.uk)

civilian observer, David Hume Pinsent. Prior to joining the Royal Aircraft Establishment, Pinsent had gained a first-class honours degree in mathematics and then studied law. Deemed unfit for active service, he found a role as a civilian test pilot. Lutyens, on the other hand, had enlisted as a Private in the 10th Battalion, Royal Fusiliers on 29 August 1914. Rapidly climbing through the ranks, he was promoted to Second Lieutenant on 15 December the same year. He went to France in 1915, serving in the Battle of the Somme, finally transferred to the Royal Flying Corps on 29 March 1917. Having completed his pilot's training at the RNAS Training Station at Vendome in France, by

This memorial to an American pilot who was killed whilst serving in the RAF can be found beside a small lane near the village of Masnières, which in turn is a few miles south of Cambrai in France. Lieutenant Theodore Rickey Hostetter was shot down on 28 September 1918, whilst flying a Sopwith Camel of 3 Squadron. He was the twenty-fifth victory of the German Ace Robert Ritter von Greim of Jagdgruppe 9. Hostetter was one of two children born to Theodore Hostetter (who died in 1902), a wealthy Pittsburgh sportsman, gambler and socialite, and his wife, Aileen Tews. The memorial was paid for by his mother. (Historic Military Press)

FROM PROPELLERS TO GLOBES REMEMBERING THE FALLEN 1914-1918

August 1917 he had been assigned to the staff of the RAE, no doubt because of his background in mechanical and electrical engineering.

It is stated that Lutyens and Pinsent were airborne in A7671 in order to carry out a series of pressure tests on its tailplane, and that it was the failure of the tailplane that caused the crash near Frimley in Surrey which claimed both of their lives. A report in the *Surrey Advertiser* of 18 May 1918, notes 'that Lieut. Lutyens was a registered pilot, quite qualified, and had flown overseas. Both Lieut. Lutyens and Mr. Pinsent had flown in the same machine many times before, and the flights had all been successful ones.

'The machine had been examined just before the flight, and everything was in as good trim as possible. A witness said the machine appeared to be flying in good condition when all at once it seemed to make a nose-dive, and immediately appeared to fall to pieces. Lieut. Lutyens death must have been instantaneous.'

Whilst Lutyens' body was recovered at the time of the crash, mystery initially surrounded the fate of Pinsent. The *Birmingham Mail* of 15 May 1918 was finally able to shed some light on the civilian observer's fate: 'The body of Mr. David Hugh [sic] Pinsent, a civilian observer … [and] the second victim of last Wednesday's aeroplane accident in West Surrey, was last night found the Basingstoke Canal at Frimley. The body of the pilot, Lieut. Lutyens, was discovered near the wreckage at the time of the accident, but despite a search no trace of Mr. Pinsent could be found until last night, when his body was recovered some distance from the spot where Lieut. Lutyens was discovered.'

○ The memorial designed by Sir Edwin Lutyens that commemorates the death of his nephew, Lieutenant Lionel Francis Derek Lutyens, in an accident on 8 May 1918. (Historic Military Press)

In another newspaper, it was noted that Pinsent's body was 'found floating in the Basingstoke Canal between Frimley and Mytchett Bridges by two officers of the London Regt. who were boating'.

Lionel Lutyens was one of five nephews that Edwin Lutyens, one of the Imperial War Graves Commission's three principal architects, lost during the First World War. A private memorial designed by Edwin marks his nephew's grave in St Michael and All Angels Churchyard in the Surrey village of Thursley. ●

○ Commemorating the death of Captain Jack Oliver Cooper RFC, this bronze plaque is mounted on the wall of a building on the south side of The Serpentine in London's Hyde Park. Oliver was flying an Royal Aircraft Factory RE7 of 21 Squadron (serial number 2388), with Lieutenant Alfred Vernon Oliver-Jones as his observer, when it was shot by anti-aircraft fire near Beaulencourt during a bombing mission on 21 July 1916. (Courtesy of Robert Mitchell)

NOTES
1. The total number of casualties varies from source to source. The National Army Museum, for examples, states that, 'during the war, the Royal Flying Corps, the Royal Naval Air Service and Royal Air Force lost 9,378 men'.
2. McCrery, Nigel, *Into Touch: Rugby Internationals Killed in the Great War* (Pen & Sword, Barnsley, 2014), pp.192-3.
3. For more information, see www.iancastlezeppelin.co.uk.
4. Quoted on www.historicengland.org.uk.
5. See Elliott White Springs, *War Birds: The Diary of A Great War Pilot* (Frontline Books, Barnsley, 2016), introduction by Mark Hillier, p.xii.
6. Lewis, Cecil, *Sagittarius Rising* (Peter Davis, London, 1936), p.11.

REMEMBERING THE FALLEN **101**

A HISTORY OF CONFLICT
BRITAIN AT WAR

Your favourite magazine is also available digitally.
DOWNLOAD THE APP NOW FOR FREE.

FREE APP
with sample issue
IN APP ISSUES £3.99

SUBSCRIBE & SAVE
Monthly £2.99
6 issues £19.99
12 issues £34.99

SEARCH: Britain at war

Read on your iPhone & iPad, Android, PC & Mac, kindle fire, Blackberry, Windows 10

ALSO AVAILABLE FOR DOWNLOAD

SEARCH AVIATION NEWS
FREE APP with sample issue
IN APP ISSUES £3.99

SEARCH FLYPAST
FREE APP with sample issue
IN APP ISSUES £3.99

FREE Aviation Specials App

IN APP ISSUES £3.99

Simply download to purchase digital versions of your favourite aviation specials in one handy place! Once you have the app, you will be able to download new, out of print or archive specials for less than the cover price!

SEARCH: Aviation Specials

How it Works.
Simply download the Britain at War app and receive your sample issue completely free. Once you have the app, you will be able to download new or back issues (from December 2011 onwards) for less than newsstand price or, alternatively, subscribe to save even more!

Don't forget to register for your Pocketmags account. This will protect your purchase in the event of a damaged or lost device. It will also allow you to view your purchases on multiple platforms.

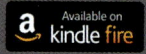

Available on iTunes · Available on the App Store · Available on Google play · Available on BlackBerry · Available on kindle fire · Available on PC, Mac & Windows10

Available on PC, Mac, Blackberry, Windows 10 and kindle fire from **pocketmags.com**

Requirements for app: registered iTunes account on Apple iPhone, iPad or iPod Touch. Internet connection required for initial download. Published by Key Publishing Ltd. The entire contents of these titles are © copyright 2018. All rights reserved. App prices subject to change. 656/18

THE THIEPVAL MEMORIAL REMEMBERING THE FALLEN 1914-1918

THE THIEPVAL MEMORIAL

Towering over the landscape of the Somme battlefield, the Thiepval Memorial bears the names of more than 72,000 officers and men of the United Kingdom and South African forces who have no known grave.

The Battle of the Somme in 1916 resulted in almost half a million British and Commonwealth casualties. Of these, more than 95,000 were killed or listed as missing, of whom 73,367 have no known grave, despite the battlefield being searched at least six times for lost bodies. It was to remember these soldiers, and the others of the United Kingdom and South African forces who died in the Somme sector before 20 March 1918, that the largest, and the last, of the memorials to Great Britain's First World War missing was built – the Thiepval Memorial to the Missing of the Somme.

The task of designing the Thiepval Memorial fell to the architect Sir Edwin Lutyens. One of the first considerations facing the Imperial War Graves Commission had been the question of where to erect the memorial. Lutyens himself had first suggested that the structure should straddle the Thiepval to Authuille road, rather in the style of the Menin Gate at Ypres. Another option had been to place it on the exact site of the old Thiepval Château which was destroyed in the fighting. This idea was discounted by virtue of the fact that a large number of burials from the various first aid posts established in and around the Château already existed at this spot.[1]

As it transpired, it was cost, above other considerations, which led to the selection of a point just south of Thiepval village and 220 yards to the south-east of the château. This was because by the time plans had been drawn up and work on the memorial was due to begin, the effects of a global economic downturn and the lingering legacy of Britain's First World War debt were making themselves felt. By positioning the memorial higher up the slope of the Thiepval ridge there was no need for a 'high and expensive podium' for the structure. It also allowed for a much shorter access road. Similar concessions also led to Lutyens reducing the size of the memorial's final design by about twenty-five per cent. As well as the financial savings that this brought, it also meant that the height of the Thiepval Memorial would be just below that of the Arc de Triomphe.

Lutyens' final plans for the memorial were submitted in January 1928 and permission for construction to go ahead was finally granted on 12 April 1928. His final design was of a base of massive square pillars, a towering series of arches, the whole in red brick and stone, which would dominate the countryside for miles around.

◉ The Thiepval Memorial and, in the foreground, the Thiepval Anglo-French Cemetery, pictured from the air. (Courtesy of Aero Photo Studio)

REMEMBERING THE FALLEN 103

REMEMBERING THE FALLEN 1914-1918 THE THIEPVAL MEMORIAL

The concept for the memorial that was eventually built at Thiepval, sketched on a sheet of Lutyens's office writing paper. A timber model of this design, painted red and white, was displayed at the Royal Academy's summer exhibition in 1925. (Courtesy of the CWGC)

Construction work underway at Thiepval in the 1930s. (Courtesy of the CWGC)

Building work began the following year – but the builders soon encountered problems. At Thiepval, as elsewhere on the Western Front, the Germans had constructed numerous deep and solid dug-outs. When the foundations for the memorial were being dug in May 1929, to a depth of twenty-four feet so that the footings sat on solid chalk, the tunnels to three German dug-outs, part of the defenders' second line of defences, were discovered, still stocked with boxes of unexploded bombs and shells. Just before this work began, the site had again been cleared, at which point the debris of war uncovered was found to include the bodies of six German soldiers and an unexploded 15-inch shell.[2]

The building work was completed in early 1932. The result was a massive stepped pyramidal form of intersecting arches that culminates in a towering eighty-foot high central arch. Clad in brick, the memorial's sixteen piers are faced with white Portland stone upon which the names of the missing are engraved. The original facing bricks came from a brick works near Lille – over ten million bricks and 100,000 cubic feet of stone were used in the construction at an estimated cost of £117,000 (some £6m today). The whole structure sits on a ten-foot-thick 'raft' that was formed from 12,000 tons of concrete.

A WASTE OF MONEY?

As the memorial neared completion, it was decided that an Anglo-French Cemetery should be laid out in front of the memorial to symbolise the joint efforts and suffering of both armies during the war. Each country provided the remains of 300 of its soldiers. Of the 300 Commonwealth burials in the cemetery, 239 are unidentified. The bodies were found between December 1931 and March 1932, from as far north as Loos and as far south as Le Quesnel.

At the time, however, not everyone was in favour of the memorial – not least among some former soldiers who, deriding the structure's cost and scale, perceived it as a waste of money, a sum that was better spent on those veterans still suffering the effects of the Great War.

Nevertheless, despite such complaints, there was never any question about the completion of the great monument, and plans were put in place to hold the memorial's official unveiling ceremony on 16 May 1932. This, however, had to be

LISTED BY REGIMENT

The names on the panels are grouped by regiment and rank; the battalions of the London Regiment, with their 4,300 names, are divided whilst all the other regiments are carved without further sub-division. After the London Regiment, the next five regiments with the highest number of names recorded are the Northumberland Fusiliers (2,920); the Royal Fusiliers (City of London Regiment) (2,500); the King's Liverpool Regiment (2,140); the Middlesex Regiment (1,920); and the Manchester Regiment (1,870).

In all eleven regiments are represented by lists of 1,500 or more casualties. In fact, approximately one third of those commemorated are from these eleven regiments. Although the memorial covers the period from March 1915 until 20 March 1918, approximately ninety per cent of those commemorated died during the 1916 battle.

Records show that the age range of those commemorated on the memorial is between 15 and 53-years-old. The average age of the dead is 25. At the same time, every military rank from Private to Lieutenant Colonel is represented. In total, there are over 2,800 officers listed.

Another view of the structure being built. The memorial is actually hollow, built of engineering brick with the large flat roof sections created by set-backs constructed of reinforced concrete. (Courtesy of the CWGC)

104 REMEMBERING THE FALLEN

THE THIEPVAL MEMORIAL REMEMBERING THE FALLEN 1914-1918

Sir Fabian Ware, the founder of the Imperial War Graves Commission, talking to the Prince of Wales at the Thiepval Memorial's unveiling ceremony on 1 August 1932. Sir Edwin Lutyens can be standing behind and to the left. (Courtesy of the CWGC)

The President of France, Albert Lebrun, speaking during the Thiepval Memorial's unveiling ceremony. (National Library of France)

postponed after the President of the French Republic, Paul Doumer, was assassinated by a Russian émigré on 7 May. The inauguration finally went ahead on the afternoon of 1 August 1932, in the presence of the Prince of Wales and the new French President, Albert Lebrun.

When it was dedicated, the memorial's sixteen piers bore the names of 73,357 officers and men in lettering chiseled by Macdonald Gill on fifty-six stone wall panels – the newly published registers, on the other hand, contained the particulars of 73,077 dead. Between the carving of the panels and the first edition of the registers, the remains of 280 men had been found, usually as the woods and remaining tracts of devastated land on the Somme were cleared or brought under the plough.

A French Guard of Honour drawn up by the Thiepval Memorial during the unveiling ceremony on 1 August 1932. (Courtesy of the CWGC)

THE INAUGURATION

The dedication service, held in English and French, duly went ahead, and the event was widely covered in the press. It was even broadcast by the BBC to listeners both in the United Kingdom and across the Empire. In Australia, it was the first major overseas event to be re-broadcast from a shortwave transmission.

Amongst the reports published around the world was the following detailed account: 'The Prince of Wales as president of the Imperial War Graves Commission to-day unveiled the British memorial at Thiepval to the missing who fell in the battles of the Somme. This is the last and greatest of the War memorials erected by the Imperial War Graves Commission in France [and] … with the unveiling of the Thiepval Memorial the commemoration of the British soldiers who fell in France and Belgium in the Great War is complete …

'The memorial stands like a castle, massive and magnificent, on the highest point of the Sommne battlefield – the Thiepval Ridge, of glorious and terrible memories, that cost more bitter fighting to approach, more blood to win, than

REMEMBERING THE FALLEN 105

REMEMBERING THE FALLEN 1914-1918 THE THIEPVAL MEMORIAL

○ Located a short distance from the Thiepval Memorial is the Ulster Memorial Tower. It stands on the site of the Schwaben Redoubt, a strongly fortified German position on the front line during the Battle of the Somme, and opposite Thiepval Wood from where the 36th (Ulster) Division made its historic charge on 1 July 1916. Dedicated on 19 November 1921, the Tower was the first official memorial to be erected on the Western Front. A replica of a well-known Ulster landmark, Helen's Tower, which stands on the Dufferin and Ava Estate at Clandeboye, County Down, this memorial commemorates all those from Ulster who served in the First World War, and in particular those who gave their lives and the officers and men of the 36th (Ulster) Division. (Shutterstock)

The Prince of Wales arrived at the memorial at 15.00 hours to be welcomed by Sir Fabian Ware and other British officials. A few minutes later, they were joined by President Lebrun and his key ministers. The group passed between long lines of French colonial horsemen before inspecting the guard of honour from the 51st French Infantry Regiment and took up their positions on a tribune on the wide lawn at the foot of the memorial.

THE PRINCE'S ADDRESS

After the first prayers and a hymn, Sir Fabian Ware invited the Prince of Wales to perform the unveiling ceremony. The latter duly stepped up to the rostrum and delivered his address, not only to the multitude of official personages and relatives of the fallen who stood before him, but also to a countless audience in every part of the Empire. After acknowledging the sacrifices suffered by the French during the four years of war, the Prince continued:

'It is fitting that the crowning stone of the work of our Imperial War Graves Commission should be laid in France; it is fitting that

any other shell-mangled, bullet-swept piece of ground that British troops had defied death to conquer. It towers like a citadel above the windy slopes, corn-covered and sunny to-day, towards which the British divisions hurled themselves in a frenzy of sacrifice 16 years ago, fighting their way up from the grisly morasses of the Ancre, gaining a precarious foothold on firmer ground, losing it again, crawling their way over the bodies of their comrades through murderous woods and gas-poisoned ruins towards the fortress on the hill where their names may now be read.

'On its great piers, above the names of the missing, are French names which have gone into British history, Beaumont Hamel, Mametz, Delville Wood. Pozieres, Le Transloy, Flers. From the observer on the ground the old scars are hidden now by a cloak of vegetation, but from the summit of the memorial, where the British and French flags fly together, the trench lines can still be seen spread like a ghostly network over the fields.'

○ Another picture showing the construction of the Thiepval Memorial underway. (Courtesy of the CWGC)

this, the last of their memorials, should bear a tribute to the Armies of France as well as to our own; and it is most fitting that, in the shadow of this memorial to our own missing of the Somme, soldiers of France and the British Empire should lie side by side to remind all men, to-day and in the years to come, of our joint losses in the Great War, our common sacrifice of two and a half million of our finest manhood. For on no other Allies did the cost of victory fall so heavily; and it was on French soil that the largest number of our soldiers fell, and in the kindly land of France have been given a resting place ...

'I have with me to-day, representatives of those sister nations which form the British Empire; in the same generous spirit in which they fought side by side, they have joined together, in free partnership, in this duty. It is the first and, I often think, an invaluable example of the way in which

○ Looking up at the Thiepval Memorial's vast central arch. The names of the casualties listed on the memorial are carved on Portland Stone panels such as that in the bottom right corner of this view. The sixteen piers formed have sixty-four stone-panelled sides carved with the names. Above are stone laurel wreaths naming significant places on the Somme battlefields of 1915 to March 1918. (Joaquin Ossorio Castillo/Shutterstock)

THE THIEPVAL MEMORIAL REMEMBERING THE FALLEN 1914-1918

The Thiepval Memorial and, in the foreground, the Thiepval Anglo-French Cemetery with the Cross of Sacrifice. The latter is normally found in cemeteries containing forty or more burials. (Jon Nicholls Photography/Shutterstock)

free nations under a common Crown may cooperate for a common object. I am very proud of the result – probably the biggest single piece of constructive work we have accomplished since the War. In France, in Belgium, in Italy, and wherever else throughout the world our Armies fought, the names of our dead are individually recorded on the headstones marking their graves, on memorials to the missing such as this, and in the volumes of the printed Registers – more than one million names, at least 90 per cent of them, those of men who before August, 1914, were civilians, strange to arms.

'These names, and the names of the even greater host of the dead of France; the names of the dead of other nations who fought with us and of those who fought against us-all these, so long as we remember them, shall testify against the past, and shall call us to a better civilization, in which it will be at last realized that the only sure happiness for each individual nation is to be found in the peace and prosperity of the whole world.'

THE WAIL OF THE PIPES

The Prince's address was followed by that of the French President, after which came the climax of the ceremony: 'The notes of the Last Post rang out from among the pillars, and the colours of the British Legion and French ex-soldiers massed on either side of the main steps of the memorial sank slowly in salute. There followed a moment of utter silence. In the great empty archways, with a bank of grey cloud beyond it throwing its sunlit masonry into clear relief, the stone of remembrance stood like an altar, simple and undecorated, a symbol of absence and of loss.

'The wail of pipes followed the bugles, and slowly the pipers moved across that artificial skyline, their tartans flying in the wind. Then three buglers of the Durham Light Infantry appeared before the stone of remembrance and sounded the Reveille; and as they did so the Union Jack and the Tricolour broke from twin flagstaffs on the summit of the memorial, brilliant in the sunshine against their background of grey cloud.'

Sadly, as we all know only too well, the Prince's hopes for a world of peace would be dashed within just a few short years.

An aerial photograph of the Thiepval Memorial's unveiling ceremony on 1 August 1932. The French Guards of Honour, both foot and mounted, can be seen at the bottom of the photograph. Note the shell-cratered field just beyond the memorial. (Courtesy of the CWGC)

NOTES
1. Gavin Stamp, *The Memorial to the Missing of the Somme* (Profile Books, London, 2007), p.130.
2. Gerald Gliffon, *Somme 1916: A Battlefield Companion* (The History Press, Stroud, 2009) p.428.

REMEMBERING THE FALLEN 107

REMEMBERING THE FALLEN 1914-1918 A SECOND WORLD WAR

A SECOND WORLD WAR

It was not unusual for German servicemen and women to have a camera with them during the events of 1939 and 1940, as well as the occupations that followed. These cameras allowed them to capture their visits to the cemeteries and memorials of the Great War.

It was believed that the Paris Peace Conference in 1919 would establish a new world order, one in which international disputes would be solved by negotiations and not by war. The conflict of 1914-1918 was to be, most hoped, the war to end war.

Twenty years later, however, Europe was again plunged into a global conflict, one in which the German armed forces swept across many of the battlefields of the Great War. Some of the memorials and sites commemorating the events on the Western Front between 1914 and 1918 therefore found themselves on the front line once again, in many cases quite literally.

As the following images reveal, they were also subjected to a new group of inquisitive visitors – the personnel of Hitler's armed forces.

○ German personnel from Infanterie-Regiment 480 arriving at the Ferme de Navarin War Memorial during the Blitzkrieg in 1940. Situated twenty-eight miles east of Reims, this imposing memorial is a combined monument and ossuary, within which lie the remains of 10,000 soldiers who fell on the plains of Champagne.
(All images Historic Military Press)

A SECOND WORLD WAR REMEMBERING THE FALLEN 1914-1918

◎ German personnel visiting the Vimy Ridge Memorial soon after it fell behind German lines in 1940. The memorial is still covered by some of the boarding put up to protect its structure.

◎ German servicemen pictured visiting the Canadian National Memorial on Vimy Ridge in the summer of 1940.

◎ German troops pictured inspecting the preserved trenches in the grounds of the Canadian National Memorial on Vimy Ridge. The white sign on the background points out that they are on the original German front line of 1917.

◎ A German staff car pictured in front of the Château-Thierry American Monument. Designed by Paul Cret, the memorial is located on a hill two miles west of Château-Thierry, France, and commands a wide view of the valley of the Marne River. It commemorates the sacrifices and achievements of American and French forces before and during the Aisne-Marne and Oise-Aisne offensives.

REMEMBERING THE FALLEN 109

REMEMBERING THE FALLEN 1914-1918 A SECOND

○ A soldier of Infanterie-Division 30 pictured in front of Godezonne Farm Cemetery in the summer of 1940. The cemetery was made in the garden of Godezonne Farm between February and May 1915 by the 2nd Royal Scots and the 4th Middlesex.

○ A group of German soldiers pictured by the entrance to the Drachenhöhle in the summer of 1940. Also known as the Dragon's Cavern, Caverne du Dragon, or Dragon's Hole, the Drachenhöhle is the site of an old stone quarry which became an underground barracks in the Great War. From 1915 it was taken over by German troops who installed electricity, gun positions and dressing stations. The French recaptured much of the site in June 1917.

○ Evidence of the fighting during the Battle for France in 1940 that could be seen at the Notre Dame de Lorette French War Memorial and War Cemetery, also known as the Ablain St.-Nazaire French Military Cemetery.

○ Two German servicemen pictured by the entrance to Serre Road Cemetery No.2 on the Somme. The original album indicates that the men are from Infanterie-Regiment 72 and that the picture was taken in 1940.

○ A German soldier examines graves in the IWGC's (later the CWGC) Canadian Cemetery No.2 at Neuville-St. Vaast, France, in the summer of 1940. Note the battle-damaged headstones. The Cemetery is located close to the Canadian National Memorial on Vimy Ridge.

○ German servicemen by the memorial to Field Marshal Sir Douglas Haig which was located in the Place du Théâtre in Montreuil sur Mer. Montreuil was the headquarters of the British Army in France from March 1916 until April 1919. Upon the death of Haig in 1928, a subscription was set up by the townsfolk for the purpose of erecting an equestrian statue in his memory; the Field Marshal had a penchant for riding through the Montreuil countryside on horseback. The statute was pulled down by the Germans – as seen here – following France's surrender. After the war the people of Montreuil recovered the original mould from the sculptor, Paul Landowski, and recast a new one.

ND WORLD WAR REMEMBERING THE FALLEN 1914-1918

◉ A German soldier pictured beside the Tank Corps Memorial at Pozières.

◉ A pair of German soldiers pose for the camera in front of the Thiepval Memorial on the Somme.

◉ Not every Great War memorial in France survived the German occupation in the Second World War. This is the monument to the arrival of the American Expeditionary Force in France, and, more specifically Saint Nazaire, in 1917. The monument was unveiled and dedicated on 26 June 1926. It was blown up following the German occupation of the port – here German soldiers are using ladders and scaffolding to place explosive charges against the structure.

◉ The moment that the demolition charges on the Saint Nazaire monument are detonated. It was rebuilt after the Second World War using the original model, which was in the possession of the sculptor's daughter, as a guide.

◉ German servicemen pictured standing in Neuville-sous-Montreuil Indian Cemetery. The Indian Cemetery was made between December 1914 and March 1916 by the Lahore Indian General Hospital. The cemetery contains twenty-five burials and commemorations of the First World War, including a memorial panel to three soldiers whose bodies were cremated in accordance with their faith.

REMEMBERING THE FALLEN 1914-1918 A SECO

○ German soldiers amongst what appears to be the remains of a Belgian defensive position, including ammunition boxes, set up in the Menin Gate at Ypres during the Blitzkrieg in 1940.

○ German soldiers repairing war damage in front of the Menin Gate in Ypres following the fighting there in 1940.

○ This memorial to the raids on Zeebrugge and Ostend in 1918, a surviving section of the bows of HMS *Vindictive*, used to be located near the bridge at the end of the De Smet-De Naeyer Avenue in Ostend (where this image was presumably taken), but since 2014 has been repositioned on the eastern jetty of Ostend Harbour.

○ On 1 June 1940, Hitler flew from Feldflugplatz Odendorf to Brussels-Evere aerdrome. From Brussels, he then set out on a two-day tour of Belgium and northern France, visiting a number of the locations he had served at during the First World War. On 1 June his route took in Brussels, Gent, Ypres, Langemarck and Menen. He spent the night at Brigode Castle at Annapes, France, having visited Lille en route. On 2 June, having departed the castle at 08.30 hours, his route continued through northern France, and included stops at Vimy, Arras and Cambrai.

○ A group of German soldiers inspecting a surviving British Mark IV Female tank, No.2648, near Fort de la Pompelle, Reims during the summer of 1940.

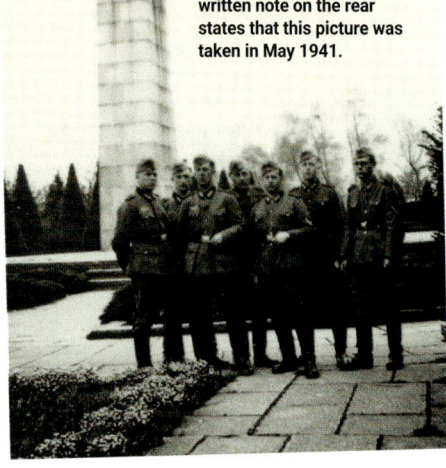

○ The Saint Julien Memorial, a Canadian war memorial and small commemorative park located in the village of Saint-Julien, near Langemark in Belgium, forms the backdrop for this group photograph. A handwritten note on the rear states that this picture was taken in May 1941.

○ A group of German soldiers at the entrance to Sillery French National Cemetery. Also known as the Nécropole Nationale de Sillery, it is at Bellevue, to the south-east of Reims close to the river Vesle. A large and typical French military cemetery, it was laid out between 1923 and 1933, and contains the bodies of 11,259 French soldiers, of whom 5,548 are in an ossuary.

○ Personnel of Panzerjäger-Abteilung 230 (Pz.Jg.Abt. 230) pictured at Fort Douaumont, Verdun, in the summer of 1940. This is the 155mm machine-gun turret position on the top of the Fort. Fort Douaumont was the largest and highest fort on the ring of nineteen large defensive forts protecting the city of Verdun.

KEEPING THE NAMES ALIVE **REMEMBERING THE FALLEN 1914-1918**

KEEPING THE NAMES ALIVE

Though the years have passed, neither the glory nor the memory of those who fought and died for their country has faded.

More than 100 years have passed since the start of the First World War. Since then a second global conflict saw death and destruction on a far greater scale. There have been other wars in many parts of the world in more recent times. Yet the desire to remember the men and women who lost their lives has not diminished and has even evolved and adapted as society and technology has changed.

We still see the marches in towns and cities around the UK and abroad on Remembrance Sunday. The two minutes' silence remains as poignant today as it ever did. Most elements of 'Poppy Day' remain little changed from the past, though the array of medals on the veterans' breasts are of more recent vintage.

It is possible, that as the years passed since 1918 such scenes of remembrance might have disappeared just as the survivors of the First World War grew fewer in number, had it

○ Children place flowers on graves during the annual ceremony to honour those Canadians buried in Shorncliffe Military Cemetery. During the First World War a number of Canadian military establishments were centred on Shorncliffe and the cemetery, which is the property of the Ministry of Defence, contains 471 First World War burials, more than 300 of them Canadian. (Department of National Defence/Library and Archives Canada)

○ The City of Portsmouth's War Memorial, which is located in Guildhall Square, being unveiled on 19 October 1921. (Historic Military Press)

not been for the Second World War which gave Britain and the Commonwealth another generation to offer their collective gratitude to. Remembrance, therefore, has continued to have relevance throughout the decades.

CARVED IN STONE

The most permanent, and personal, reminder of individual loss is, of course, that person's grave. While the memory of their deeds might not have faded, the headstones marking their final resting place often have – the passage of time, the attrition of the elements, and accidental and intentional damage all taking their toll. In all its forms, nothing is more important in terms of remembrance than keeping the headstones and the memorials of the killed and missing in legible condition – quite genuinely keeping their names alive.

From the very outset, the inscriptions on the CWGC headstones and memorials was intended to be a 'monumental inscription

… designed to be a record for those who care to search for it rather than an announcement to the world'.

According to the standards set by the CWGC itself, inscriptions should be legible from a distance of two paces from the headstone, and the badge should be recognisable from a distance of two paces and legible from one pace. Monumental inscriptions 'should be capable of being read in reasonable light conditions, with normal vision, and at a reasonable viewing distance by persons who care to pause and reflect'.

In the run-up to the centenary of the First World War, the CWGC found that a great many of the inscriptions no longer met such criteria. This presented the CWGC with the immense task of bringing thousands of them back up to the required standard – a process that will take an estimated twenty-eight years and cost in the region of £15 million. This process starts by sanding down the entire headstone followed by the re-

REMEMBERING THE FALLEN 113

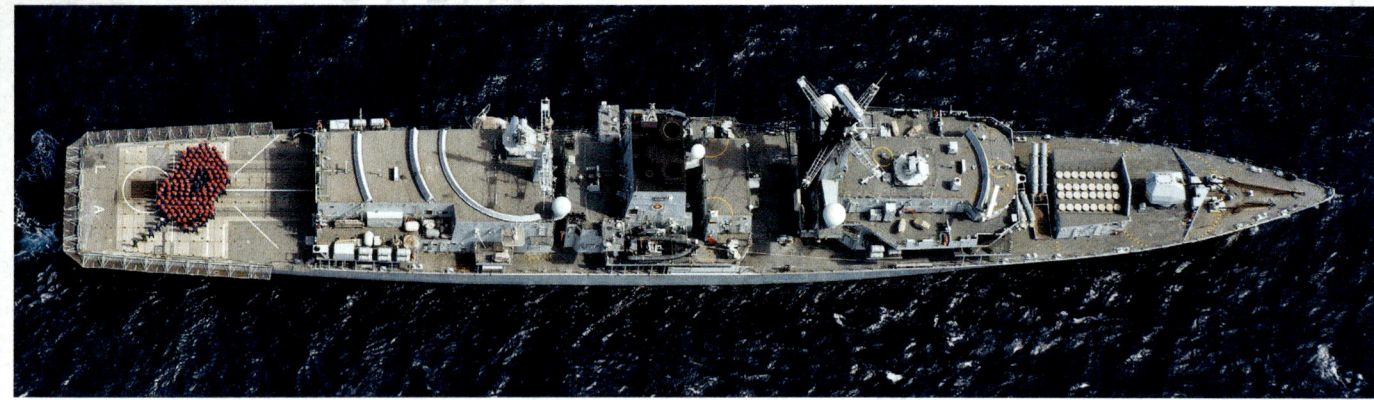

REMEMBERING THE FALLEN 1914-1918 KEEPING THE NAMES ALIVE

○ The crew of the Type 23 frigate HMS *Lancaster* form a giant red poppy as an act of Remembrance whilst at sea. (MoD/Crown Copyright, 2018)

engraving of the inscription and any insignia by hand, using a fine drill that is powered by compressed air. To finish, a fine sanding machine is used to smooth down the whole headstone. To achieve this, the Commission has fourteen stone masons who, between them, restore headstones at a rate of around six per day.

Such a phenomenal undertaking demonstrates the importance which is still attached to maintaining the memory of those lost in the First World War. As the Commission's spokesman, Peter Francis, made clear: 'We believe that an eroded inscription is a brave man or woman forgotten and that is unacceptable. Indeed, if just one name is allowed to disappear or fade into obscurity, we will all have failed in our debt to the fallen.'

Time, on the other hand, has had the beneficial effect of allowing the establishment of other permanent reminders of the sacrifices of the past. The magnificent National Memorial Arboretum is an outstanding example of this. There have

○ A member of Commonwealth War Graves Commission staff restoring the headstone of a Great War casualty, in this case that of Private 256265 George Lawrence Price in St Symphorien Military Cemetery near Mons. Private Price is generally accepted to have been the last Commonwealth soldier killed in action during the First World War. (Courtesy of the CWGC)

been other inventive creations which have also made their mark, possibly the most notable in recent times has been the ceramic poppy display 'Blood Swept Lands and Seas of Red' which was unveiled at the Tower of London in 2014. Around the world, amongst the combatant nations, remembrance projects have blossomed, with the showing of films, the creation of photographic databases, the collection of memoirs and archives, and an online commemoration by the Royal British Legion the name of which exemplifies all that the act of remembrance signifies, 'Everyone Remembered'.

This year, 2018, Remembrance Day will see ceremonies on a grand scale. The traditional march past will be extended to include a 'People's Procession', applications to participate in which were long ago filled, such was the demand from the general public to demonstrate their support. An appeal has also been made for bells to be rung throughout the world to celebrate the moment when the guns finally fell silent – just as they did in 1918.

So, as the evocative notes of the Last Post reverberate around cenotaphs and memorials throughout the length and breadth of the UK and across the world on the eleventh hour of the eleventh day of the eleventh month of 2018, the words uttered and echoed in every tongue 'We will remember them' will be no idle claim. ●

○ The Royal British Legion's Never Forget Memorial which was unveiled at the National Memorial Arboretum, Alrewas, Staffordshire, in 2014. The National Memorial Arboretum is the United Kingdom's year-round national site of Remembrance. (Caron Badkin/Shutterstock)